Dawn Wakes in the East

Dawn wakes in the east.
Don't say we are marching early.
Though we stomp over all these green hills
we are not yet old,
and from here the land is a wonder.
Mao Tse-tung

HARPER & ROW, PUBLISHERS

Wakes in the East

Audrey Topping

New York, Evanston, San Francisco, London

In memory of Inga Marie Horte Ronning, my mother

DAWN WAKES IN THE EAST

Illustrations copyright © 1973 by Audrey Topping

Production coordinated by Chanticleer Press, Inc., New York
Printed and bound by Amilcare Pizzi, S.p.A., Milan, Italy

First Edition

Standard Book Number: 06-014328-2

Library of Congress Catalog Card Number: 72-9162

Calligraphy by Jeanyee Wong
Designed by Gayle Jaeger

Prologue

序词

Early Enchantment
with China

In April 1971 I walked across the narrow railroad bridge extending from Lo Wu in Hong Kong's New Territories to Shum Chun in the People's Republic of China. It was the eighth trip to China that my family had made during the last eighty years, the third for me.

I had no more than stepped across the border when I felt it happening again. I could feel the enchantment of China seeping into my whole being. The whole world seemed new and more colorful. I looked at my father, Chester Ronning, and my sister, Sylvia Cassady, who were traveling with me, and saw it happening to them too. The bridge is no more than fifty yards long but we walked into a different world—a world that has attracted my family since the late 1800s and intrigued me since I was old enough to remember.

My curiosity about China was first stirred when I was about two and was told by my sister Meme and brother Alton that they had been born in China and I had only been born in Camrose, Alberta, Canada.

Although they seemed to accept this with incredible nonchalance, I was filled with wonder and envy. Because Meme and Alton were a few years older than myself I believed them completely when Alton told me he was digging a hole to China and Meme informed me that China lay just beyond the spruce trees we could see on our eastern horizon.

The first song I learned to sing was "Jesus Loves Me" in Chinese and our bedtime stories consisted of our parents' adventures in China. Rainy afternoons were spent in the attic looking at old photos of China and dressing in ancient Chinese robes stored in trunks.

The ultimate bliss was to cuddle into our parents' double bed under a huge black brocade Chinese robe lined with a silky Mongolian goatskin. The fur was so long we could bury our mandarin oranges in it while we asked Mom to tell us about China.

China filled my mother with fear and dread. We loved to listen to the stories of how she fought with the spiders and scorpions and how she once met up with a centipede so big she was afraid to step on it. Instead she attacked it with a butcher knife, but when she cut it up all the parts started to crawl away. We would squeal in horror and crawl deeper under the goatskin.

I am still amazed how my mother, who was a beautiful and cautious woman, managed to survive seven years in China, most of them spent in Fancheng, in the interior of China, from 1922 to 1927, and another two in Nanking from 1946 to 1948. My parents were there during the tumultuous times of the 1920–1927 "Great Revolution," when China was dominated by the warlords. It was made even more difficult because of the responsibility for their three small children, Sylvia, Alton and Meme. The family was forced to flee in 1927 when the Chinese turned dangerously antiforeign and the British consul ordered all foreigners to leave.

They escaped by sailing down the Han River to Hankow in a freight junk, called a *pien tsu*. The captain and the crew of the ship were members of the Red Spear Society, which was a revolutionary group organized to protect the boat people from the warlords, marauding soldiers and roving bandits. At Shayang, which was about halfway from Fancheng, they came to an S-turn in the river. There they met boats coming upriver from Hankow. The boats had been fired on by bandits and bodies of the sailors still lay on the bloody decks. The captain of Dad's boat refused to go any farther and they were forced to dock in Shayang. After two days of futile attempts at persuasion, Dad left the family hiding in the hold while he and a friend set off to find the telegraph office and send word of their delay to the mission in Hankow. Having sent the message, they stopped in a teahouse for some tea and buns. Before long a group of hostile students came in.

"Look at those foreign devils," they shouted. "Destroy the foreign devils. Down with imperialism."

On impulse, Dad jumped on the table and shouted in the local accent:

"You are absolutely right! Down with foreign imperialists. Let us destroy them!" As they listened in amazement, he continued: "That is exactly why I want to go down the river and across the Pacific to attack them from the other side. Together we can crush the imperialists!"

The mood of the students changed immediately. They escorted the foreigners back to their boat and persuaded the captain to continue the journey. As they set off, the students wished them a peaceful journey.

Mom remembered this trip as a terrible experience. Dad remembers it as a great adventure, and his first request when he returned to Fancheng forty-four years later was to sail the Han River in a *pien tsu*.

The difference in attitude was partly because my father was born in China, spent the first thirteen years of his life there and speaks the language fluently. It was also the second time he had been forced to flee China because of revolution. The first time was with his parents during the Boxer Rebellion in 1900. This was in the reign of the "Imperial Manchus" after the empress dowager put out an edict to kill all foreigners.

My grandparents, Hannah Rorem and Halvor Ronning, both Americans of Norwegian ancestry, were among the first Lutheran missionaries to go to China. They arrived in Hankow on December 8, 1891, and with them was Halvor Ronning's sister, Miss Thea Ronning. Halvor and Hannah were married three weeks later and moved across the Yangtze River to Wuchang. Two months later Halvor wrote a letter to his mission society in Red Wing Seminary, Minnesota, which gives a vivid description of conditions in old China.

Wuchang, February 4, 1892—We were on our way to greet the world's largest nation, the walled-in China, the "heavenly kingdom." The Lord be praised, we are now permitted to enter the open port, and behold 400,000,000 heathen.

We find ourselves in the very heart of this remarkable kingdom. Here lie the cities Hankow and Han-yang on one side of the river and Wuchang on the other. It is in the latter that I now have erected my tabernacle. Come in, come in, and sit down! Here I am sitting in my fur coat writing. Though it is in the middle of the winter and there is no snow, and the fields are green, it is still very cold in this miserable house. It is almost as if I sat out of doors. The dust lies thick on everything and when the wind blows through the open walls and the paper window, I can hardly see from one end of my cell to the other.

Brethren, I am not dissatisfied with my quarters; no, I am happy and thank the Lord that everything is better than we might have expected. When I think of Jesus, who was the Son of God, who had not where to lean His head, I am rich and have it comfortable.

Let us take a trip into the city. How I wish it might be a reality. Crowds in the narrow streets. Low, tumble-down houses stand side by side as if steadying one another. Here stands a Chinese on the street cooking his food. At his side, one is sitting being shaved. Here some are butchering and close by one is repairing shoes. On the other side is a beggar who is busy doing away with insects in his shirt. Even more disgusting scenes present themselves. "Clear the way! Clear the way!" the carriers cry. They scream as if they were carrying the whole world on their shoulders, though they have only empty sacks. Where is that smoke coming from? I'll tell you. No Chinese house has a chimney. The smoke finds its way out where best it can. Others are more civilized and have placed the chimney through the wall and out into the street. Well, they don't know any better. "Out of the way! Out of the way!" sounds the cry again. This time some sort of an official is being carried in a chair by four men. Behind him and in front of him run a flock of dogs, pigs and children, barking, squealing and shouting. To get out of the way for such a procession, we must step into a store. Wagons are not used in the streets. Everything, including stones and logs, is carried on the shoulders. Sometimes up to forty, fifty men carry a log.

In such a noisy and congested crowd, one soon gets tired. Add to all this the intolerable smell on account of the terrible filth. But, brethren, let us not forget the suffering past as the priest and the Levite and think, I am not my brother's keeper.

We continue our walk. On account of the uncleanliness there is much of eye and skin diseases. Look at these individuals. They are half naked, with open sores. Look at that old man! Only the holes left where the eyes used to be. Further down are men and women left there half dead or dying. No, we cannot stand this anymore. Let us go down to the gate. I don't know if you can stand to look at these cut-off heads.

Let me tell you that a few days ago I dipped my pen in their blood to send a message to my brethren at Red Wing Seminary. Remember the China mission. Hurry with the Gospel to the Chinese! Let not their blood come upon you! *My heart is almost crushed when I take such a trip. I shall spare you such further sights. Let us step up on the high wall. Here we have a splendid view of the surrounding country and*

Hannah and Halvor Ronning with four of their seven children in China in 1904: (from left to right) Nelius, Chester (the author's father), Almah and baby Talbert

here the air is cleaner and fresher. The wall stretches fifteen miles around the city and has eight gates, the only places where one can leave or enter. The iron doors are closed as soon as the sun sets and are not opened before daylight. One evening I was on the point of being left outside. I prayed to God to help me and as by a miracle, I got in.

From this wall we can see some small girls creeping along the ground. They can scarcely walk as their feet have been bound and are only two or three inches long. What are they creeping here for? With a small knife they are cutting grass to still their hunger. At such a sight, I become very much depressed. . . . If I had several lives I would gladly offer them on the altar of missions.

This description of old China was generally accurate until changes were effected by the Communist Revolution of the late 1940s. If Grandfather had lived to walk the same streets we did eighty years later, his Christian heart would have rejoiced to see the changes that have taken place. He would have rejoiced even though the changes occurred by revolution and an acceptance of Marxist ideology rather than through the Christian doctrine that he advocated so strongly.

My grandparents remained in China for eight years until they left during the Boxer Rebellion. Grandfather and his family went to Norway and then to America. When things quieted down in China, they returned in 1901 to their mission. Grandmother Hannah was destined to spend the rest of her life there. She died in 1907, leaving seven children. She was buried in the mission compound, where her tombstone, along with Thea Ronning's, stands to this day. It was one of the places we visited on this last trip to China.

A year after his wife's death Grandfather returned to the United States and later decided to take his children to Canada. They traveled by covered wagon up the Edson Trail to the Peace River district of northern Alberta. There they settled on unclaimed land. The four sons established homesteads by staking their claims and clearing the land of all the trees they could physically cut. They named the area Valhalla, and although Grandfather traveled widely in the United States and Canada as an evangelist, he always returned to

Valhalla. He finally remained, farming and preaching the Gospel, until he died in 1950.

Our childhood summers were spent on Grandpa's farm, where we admired the Chinese rock gardens, steamed in the Norwegian sauna and heard even more stories about China from our uncles and aunts, who had all lived there at various times. When we returned to Camrose, we would relate our versions of these stories and overheard conversations to the neighbors. We often livened them up with snatches of make-believe Chinese. In fact, unbeknownst to our parents, we became great sources of misinformation to the good citizens of Camrose. I told my first-grade teacher that everything was opposite in China and that the people even walked backward. Meme brought an old red mandarin robe with gold embroidered dragons and huge sleeves to class and told the students that the Chinese wore it shopping so that they could carry the groceries home in their sleeves. Another time, on the request of my teacher, I brought some chopsticks to school, and with one stick in each hand I demonstrated how to use them. I have always wondered why no one contradicted us.

While Meme and I were busy educating the masses, brother Alton became a staunch defender of the Chinese cause. When the neighbor boys

called him "Chinky Chinaman" because he had been born in China, Alton would tear into them with the ferocity of a People's Hero. They soon learned to speak about the Chinese in respectful tones—at least when they were around Alton—but to this day his old friends call him "Chink."

One day when I was about five and we were visiting Grandfather in Valhalla, Alton discovered a trapdoor in the ceiling of the second story of the log house. Grandfather had long since built a new stucco house where the adults stayed, while the children slept in the old house. At that age trapdoors are to open, so we soon found a ladder and Alton climbed up, slid the door partly open and came down.

"O.K.," he said. "You go first, Audrey."

I looked at Meme.

"Go ahead," she said. "We're right behind you. Don't be afraid!"

So as usual I went first. I climbed through the dark hole, and when they were sure I was still alive, they followed.

It was pitch-dark, except for the light from the door, but as our eyes became accustomed to the light we saw a fearsome sight. There was a huge golden lacquer Buddha with glass eyes staring at us. A musty smell seeped from the carved camphor chests stacked along the sloping walls.

"Is this China?" I asked the authorities.

"Yeah!" whispered Alton. "This is China, but don't tell anyone we've been here."

That was my first trip to China. The second was eleven years later, in 1946. I went with Mother, Meme, my younger sister, Kjeryn, and my brother Harmon to join Dad, who had gone to Chungking in 1945 as a Canadian diplomat. Alton was in England in the RCAF, and Sylvia stayed in Canada to teach school.

We arrived in Shanghai in December 1946—exactly fifty-five years after my grandparents' arrival—on the *Marine Lynx*, a converted troopship that had carried us across the Pacific from San Francisco. The merging yellow waters of the Whangpoo and Yangtze rivers were teeming with ships and water craft of all types. Our ship was soon surrounded by junks and sampans loaded with hawkers and by children with outstretched hands, begging for coins. Dad met us at the gangplank and guided us through the swarms of dock workers and coolies. One grabbed Kjeryn's handbag from her shoulder and fled down the street. In a flash Dad was racing after him, followed by little brother Harmon, yelling, "Stop thief!" Soon the whole family was in hot pursuit of the robber. He took one quick look backward and the sight of these long-legged foreign devils after him was too much. He flung the bag in the air and disappeared into the crowd.

We loaded into rickshas and the sweating coolies pulled us through the cluttered streets, past the glittering shops laden with foreign imports, toward the Cathay Hotel. A slew of beggars, some with open sores on their faces, followed us. When Kjeryn, then eleven years of age, had no more coins to give them, one spat full in her face. It had been a bad day for Kjeryn. She cried out in shock and dismay, and again Dad ran over and chased the beggars away with much shouting and arm waving.

Fortunately, the hotel was only a short distance away. When we walked through the door, we stepped into a completely different world. Here was one of the most luxurious hotels in Shanghai, where only the privileged and wealthy were allowed. Chinese women in richly brocaded gowns, and smartly suited Chinese businessmen and officials, mingled with the international set. We were escorted by numerous servants through the red-carpeted corridors to our elaborate suite. Safely settled behind closed doors, we indulged in a fabulous multicourse New Year's Eve feast.

For the next two years we lived in Nanking, then Chiang Kai-shek's capital, in the diplomatic community, which included the United States Military Advisory Group. My sister Meme met and married a navy man, David Westlein, and I met a romantic and earnest young reporter, Seymour ("Top") Topping, whom I married three years later in Canada.

While in Nanking I attended the University of Nanking. More interesting than my studies were the discussions I had with the students about the Communist Revolution that was going on all around us. Most of the students were waiting with enthusiasm for the Communists to come in. Riding to school in a ricksha each morning, it was not uncommon to pass the corpses of people who had died during the night, of starvation, disease or accident. Bodies sometimes lay unclaimed for days. In the evening I would attend elaborate dinners and diplomatic balls. Observing the living standards of the ultrapoor and ultrarich soon convinced me that the revolution in China was not only necessary but inevitable.

I relate these old stories only because I believe that in order to understand New China, it is necessary to have some idea of what old China was like before the Revolution. To comprehend the advances China has made, one must realize where it started from. To compare the standard of living in China with that of the United States or Europe is a mistake we often make. To fairly assess China today, we must compare China, as the Chinese do, with their own backward past, not with our industrial present.

Like my grandparents during the Boxer Rebellion in 1900 and my parents during the Great Revolution in 1927, I was forced out of China by revolution. This time it was the Communist Revolution. I was evacuated with my mother, brother and sister in November 1948. I returned to China seventeen years, one husband and four daughters later. Top was *The New York Times*'s chief correspondent in Southeast Asia and we lived in Hong Kong. In June 1966, at the onset of the Great Proletarian Cultural Revolution, I left Top and the children in Hong Kong and traveled for three weeks to Canton, Hangchow, Shanghai, Wusih, Soochow, Nanking and Peking as a Canadian tourist.

The next trip was in April, May and June 1971. My father had received an invitation from his old friend Chou En-lai, the Premier of China, and since my mother had died in 1967 and he was alone, my sister Sylvia, Mrs. Harry Cassady, and I jumped at the chance to accompany him. The main purpose of our trip was to visit Dad's home town of Fancheng in the interior of China, but we also had the opportunity to visit Canton, Peking, Shih-chia-chuang, Hankow, Wuchang, Hanyang, Hsiangyang, Nanking, Shanghai and Hangchow.

After five weeks Top joined us in Hangchow on my birthday, May 21, with the news that our now five daughters, living in Scarsdale, New York, were all fine and had agreed that I should stay and travel with him. Dad and Sylvia went south for a week before leaving and I stayed on for another five weeks with Top. We went north to Peking and on to Shenyang and Anshan in Manchuria. Then, leaving Top at work in Peking, I traveled with some other journalists to Yenan, Taiyuan and Sian in the northwest.

I returned to China for two months, September and October, 1972. This time I went with my enthusiastic friend, Lucy Jarvis, a producer with NBC News, and a talented crew of six to help make two special documentaries on Peking. I am grateful to NBC for permission to include here some of the photographs I took on that trip.

This book contains word and picture impressions of China which I gathered while traveling over twelve thousand miles. I visited seventeen cities, took photos freely and talked to people in almost every walk of life. There are also some firsthand experiences of my father.

My main purpose, after several imaginary and four real journeys to China, is to try once again to give the good citizens of my home town in Camrose and all the other people in similar towns throughout Canada and the United States some information about and understanding of China and its people.

I am especially indebted to my father, who made the trip possible, and to Top and the girls, who let me go.

The Center—
Peking

中心・北京

[10]

OLD CATHAY

Politically and culturally, the heart of China is in Peking, for all things emanate from the capital. Where once the imperial emperors held sway, the People's Republic of China now rules. But the traditional legacy of China, deeply rooted in its people and their lives, is not forgotten. Peking blends the ancient and the modern in unique charm. The Gate of Heavenly Peace (Tien An Men) is the symbol of Peking and all of China. The famous old structure has held its silent vigil since the early Ming dynasty, when it was built as the main entrance to the "Forbidden City," which contains the Imperial Palaces where the Ming and later the Ch'ing emperors and their courts resided. The gate was reconstructed in its present form in 1651.

While the south side of the gate overlooks Tien An Men Square and modern Peking, the north side still looks upon the former Imperial Palaces and the gardens in the forecourt, which have become a People's Cultural Park. The Forbidden City has been turned into a city of museums.

Once inside the ancient vermilion walls of the palaces, "Old Cathay" becomes a reality and the bustling modern city of Peking lying outside is

[12]

forgotten. In the midst of the sculptured animals and gardens, the shimmering-roofed golden temples and the haunted rooms filled with fabulous treasures from the Middle Kingdom, one senses the cool hand of history that wrote centuries of political and private intrigue within the Forbidden City.

The palaces are divided into two main parts. The front section, which was constructed during the reign of the Ming Emperor Yung Lo from 1407 to 1420, contains the Three Big Halls with their decorative gates and courtyards. The first and largest is the Hall of Supreme Harmony (T'ai Ho Tien), often called the Hall of Golden Bells. Here the Ming and Ch'ing emperors issued edicts and celebrated special ceremonies such as birthdays, the lunar New Year, accession and winter solstice. The emperor's gilt Dragon Throne still stands in the awesome interior.

Next is the Hall of Middle Harmony (Chung Ho Tien), where the emperors received their attendants before holding ceremonies.

Third is the Hall of Preserving Harmony (Pao Ho Tien), which became the Palace of Imperial Examination, where classic scholars took the highest examination. If they passed, they became officials of the empire.

[14]

Elaborate gates and crimson corridors lead to the rear section of the Forbidden City, which is a maze of fairy tale palaces, pavilions and temples. Symbolic animals and birds in Ming yellow and celestial purple gaze down from the roof corners. This is where the emperors, princes and mandarins with their wives, concubines, children and eunuchs had their private domains.

The main palaces here are the Palace of Heavenly Purity (Ch'ien Ch'ing Kung), the Hall of Union (Chiao T'ai Tien), the Palace of Earthly Tranquillity (K'un Ning Kung) and the Six East and West Palaces.

[15]

Golden lions guard the gate to the
Treasure House in the Forbidden City,
where three large halls are filled with
priceless relics of the past. On display
are: one of sixteen pure gold bells
made in 1791, each bell marked with
the note it rings when struck: a
gold hair receptacle made in 1777 to
hold Emperor Ch'ien Lung's mother's
hair after her death; a coat of mail
made of six hundred thousand gold
and silver links (Ch'ien Lung); an
emperor's robe embroidered with coral
beads and pearls; a ceremonial saddle;
and the Jade Mountain, which weighs
five tons and which took ten years
to carve.

During the Cultural Revolution many ancient sites and tombs were excavated. This bronze galloping horse, discovered in the tomb of a general who lived during the Eastern Han Dynasty (A.D. 25–200) in Kansu province, is among the most beautiful examples of unearthed treasures now on display in the Forbidden City. Scores of other bronze horses were found in the same tomb. Here they are lined up in a ghostly procession in an ancient imperial courtyard.

[19]

The Pavilion of Eternal Spring enhances the Imperial Garden (Yu Hua Yuan), which is also in the rear section. Animal sentinels made of bronze and stone adorn the garden and guard the palaces. There are imperial dragons, golden lions, elephants, unicorns and other mythical beasts, each with its own symbolic powers to drive away evil spirits and endue the beholder with special characteristics.

Nearby the Empress Dowager Tz'u Hsi had her private rooms. The elaborate interiors and silk-curtained beds are still on exhibition. The empress was the last imperial ruler of any significance. She died in 1908 and with her died Ancient China.

Temple of Heaven

Old Cathay is still evident in the rest of Peking, which is an enchanting mixture of the old and the new. Modern Peking has grown around its historic temples, gates, palaces and ancient gardens. Many have been converted into museums or people's parks. Playgrounds and tea pavilions have been built nearby and these relics of old China are alive with children, students and sightseers.

On Sundays and holidays the Temple of Heaven Park is full of children playing in the gardens and playground while their parents explore the temples. The central structure is one of Peking's finest works of architecture, the Hall of Annual Prayer (Ch'i-nien). It was constructed by the Mings in the early fifteenth century and is where the emperors offered prayers for bountiful harvests. When our interpreter explained this, he added. "In those days they only prayed for food. Now we do something about it ourselves." But there was no scorn in his voice. To him it was a matter of progress.

An imperial golden dragon lurks on the highest point of the temple's circular ceiling, which is held up by vermilion and gold columns. The temple has recently been restored to its original colors.

[22]

[23]

A smaller hall in the same style contains an altar where offerings to heaven were made. It is encircled by the "whispering wall," which seems to catch a whisper or any small noise and carry it around its circumference, from any point of which it can be heard clearly. The marble Altar of Heaven, aligned on a north-south axis, was positioned to amplify prayers. The whole temple area was geometrically designed and is replete with mystical symbolism.

[25]

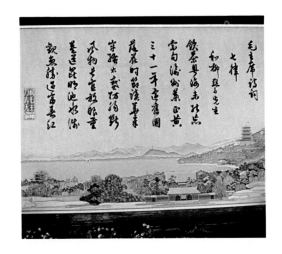

A popular excursion in Peking is to the Summer Palace about twelve miles northwest of the city. On holidays thousands come by bus, foot and truck to explore the palaces on Longevity Hill and go boating or skating on K'un Ming Lake. They bring their lunch and spend the day in the 659 acres of magnificent gardens where formerly the imperial court came to avoid the heat of the summer. Built in 1153 by Emperor Wan Yan-liang, the Summer Palace was enlarged and maintained until 1860, when European troops sacked it. The only building left intact was the bronze pagoda. The empress dowager rebuilt the Summer Palace in 1888 as her private retreat.

Since 1949 large-scale restoration work has been carried out by the People's Liberation Army and the palace is open to the public.

[26]

[27]

An elaborate marble boat standing in K'un Ming Lake near the Summer Palace serves as a reminder of the caprice of the powerful Empress Dowager Tz'u Hsi. She had the extravagant toy built with money she was given to build a navy. Perhaps if everyone had followed her example the world would be better off today. Now it is enjoyed by the people of Peking, who can stand on deck and sail imaginary seas. Inside is a mirror that reflects the rippling water, and although the boat is stationary one has the illusion of movement. One of our Chinese friends on seeing this remarked sarcastically, "She really knew how to live!"

THE GREAT WALL AND
THE MING TOMBS

A walk along the Great Wall of China
and a visit to the ancient tombs of the
Ming emperors are all in a day's trip
from Peking, but it is a journey that
takes one back centuries in time. The
Great Wall is perhaps the most formi-
dable of all Chinese historical relics,
and although its usefulness as a military barrier expired long ago, the
wall is still alive with people who
come to see this awesome monument
to China's indestructible spirit and
to walk along its ancient ramparts.

The Great Wall stretches for 1,500
miles from Chiayukuan Pass in Kansu
province in the west to Shanhaikuan
Pass in the east. It stands fifteen to
thirty feet high and is about eighteen
feet wide on top. It is said that five or
six horses can gallop abreast along the
top of the wall. League upon league, the
wall twists and turns and plunges and
climbs like the jagged spine of a menac-
ing dragon. Crushed and buried be-
neath the massive gray rocks are the
bones of thousands of slave laborers
and prisoners who died building this
military barrier. Their spirits seem to
cry in the wind and haunt the grim
watchtowers that stand, stark and four-
square, along the parapets.

The wall was first constructed during
the period of the Warring States (475–

221 B.C.), when each state built a wall of defense around its own territory. The walls were joined during the Ch'in dynasty in 221 B.C. It has been reconstructed many times since: eighteen times during the 276 years of the Ming dynasty, once by the great Genghis Khan and most recently by the present regime.

With the help of the People's Liberation Army the wall was repaired at three famous points: Pataling, Shanhaikuan and Chuyungkuan, where the only original gate still stands. It dates back to 1345, during the Mongol period.

The inside is carved with a Buddha and four celestial fairies with inscriptions in six languages.

The section most popular with tourists is thirty-seven miles from Peking. It stretches twelve miles between Nankow and Pataling. In 1971 twenty thousand guests came from over one hundred countries to walk the wall and be reminded of Mao Tse-tung's famous poem: "If we reach not the Great Wall, we are no true men." If you walk, as we did, the full length of the reconstructed part of the wall, you can see how sections have crumbled away. At Pataling, where the road passes under the wall as it heads for Inner Mongolia, visitors can lunch in the teahouses or buy ice cream, frozen ices or hot cakes from little stands set up near one of the fallen cannon that once blasted from the Great Wall.

Not far from the wall is the road called the Sacred Way, which leads to the Ming Tombs. It is guarded by rows of stone animals and human figures depicting mandarins and officials from the emperor's court. They date from the fifteenth century, as does the old gate that leads to the Ting Ling Tomb.

There are fifteen emperors buried in this area, but the most interesting site is Ting Ling because it is the only one that has been excavated, in 1956, when it was found to contain the bodies of Emperor Wan Li, his two wives and their fantastic array of treasures. A stone tablet stands inside a pavilion near the tomb. Carved into the stone are Chinese characters telling the history of the emperor's reign. Underground, near the crypt, is the heavenly throne, made of marble. It sits before a porcelain pot decorated with the blue dragon, symbol of the emperors, that was once filled with rare oils which were supposed to burn forever. The treasures that have been unearthed stand in a museum in the gardens that surround the tomb. Among them are gold and jade vessels and crowns studded with jewels and gold inlaid with the blue eye of peacock feathers.

TIEN AN MEN SQUARE

The centuries of the sometimes wise but often decadent and selfish rule of the imperial emperors ended with the fall of the Manchu dynasty in 1912. Then China suffered thirty-seven years of chaos, foreign exploitation, war and revolution. Finally, on October 1, 1949, a victorious Mao Tse-tung stood on the Gate of Heavenly Peace and with his back to the Imperial Palaces and the past, his face toward the city of Peking and the future, he proclaimed the People's Republic of China.

Now history is being made on the other side of the Gate of Heavenly Peace, in Tien An Men Square. In the center of the square a memorial to the People's Heroes rises 128 feet high. On the east stands the Museum of History, while on the west is the Great Hall of the People, where state functions, party congresses, meetings of the Assembly of People's Representatives, giant state banquets and even small private dinners take place.

Tien An Men Square is where the colorful parades and fireworks spectaculars take place on the national holidays. These are New Year's (three days for the old New Year and one for the new-calendar New Year), May Day and October 1, the anniversary of the founding of the People's Republic.

On these special occasions the Gate of Heavenly Peace, the Museum of History and the Great Hall are lit up and the square is filled with almost a million people who have gathered to watch the fantastic fireworks display. The Chinese love fireworks and each rainbow blast is greeted with claps and shrieks of enthusiasm.

Tien An Men Square is also the juncture of Peking's two main boulevards, Tung-ch'ang-an (East Eternal Peace) and Hsi-ch'ang-an (West Eternal Peace), which stretch, six lanes wide, through the middle of Peking. It is along this road that state visitors drive with their entourage from the airport to the Guest House. If the visitor is considered important enough and a friend of China, throngs of people line Ch'ang-an Boulevard and, to the accompaniment of raucous drums and clanging cymbals, wave banners and flags in an overwhelming welcoming ceremony, such as the one given to President Ceausescu of Rumania, the Empress of Iran and other state visitors.

[39]

[40]

[41]

AN EVENING WITH PREMIER CHOU EN-LAI

One evening my father, Sylvia and I were invited to a small dinner party given by Premier Chou En-lai in the Great Hall of the People. Besides a banquet hall seating five thousand and an auditorium holding ten thousand, the Great Hall has twenty-eight reception rooms, named after the various provinces of China. We dined in the Kiangsu Room, which was named after the province where Chou En-lai was born. We told him we had been impressed with the Great Hall and he asked if we had seen the Hupei Room, named after the province where my father was born. When we said no, he shrugged his shoulders and laughed. "Well, I would show it to you," he said, "but I can't remember where it is!"

Dinner with the Premier of China is not only a gourmet's delight, it is mixed with words of wisdom and wit. Every visitor leaves with his own impressions of Chou, but everyone seems to agree that he radiates intelligence and worldly charm. I found him to be a virtual prism, shooting off flashes of light in all directions, yet he possesses a calm dignity and projects an inner strength that to me reflects the face of New China itself.

I had opportunities to observe and talk with him when he was relaxed and jovial in the company of old friends like my father and when he was alert and concerned over a dinner interview with intense journalists like my husband. Much has been written about his political views and attitudes toward the world situation, but the Premier is not always serious; he also has a remarkably keen wit, a warm humor and an appealing sense of the ridiculous.

The other guests at dinner that night were our old friends Huang Hua, then ambassador-designate to Canada, and now ambassador to the United Nations, and his beautiful wife, Li-liang, now councillor to the United Nations; Ch'iao Kuan-hua, vice-foreign minister; Chang Wen-chin, director of the Foreign Ministry department in charge of Western European, North and Latin American and Oceanic affairs; and two of Premier Chou's interpreters, Chi Ch'ao-chu, a former Harvard student, and Miss T'ang Wen-sheng, who was born in New York.

Two of our companion guides, Chou Ch'iu-yeh, former ambassador to the Congo and a member of the Friendship Association, and Chu Chiu-sheng, also of the Friendship Association, now a diplomat in Canada, arrived with us.

The Premier escorted us to a scrumptious-looking round table set with blue and white porcelain, ivory chopsticks, three wineglasses at each place and an exotic display of sliced ancient eggs, spiced chicken, bean curd and other cold dishes.

He turned to Dad. "Now, there will be no protocol," he said. "We will sit according to the old Chinese custom where the honored guests sit opposite the host. These younger people don't remember the gracious old customs as we do."

We sat down and Chou raised his glass of mou-t'ai in a toast. "Let us drink to old friendships," he said. Mou-t'ai is a white liquor made of sorghum, the waters of the Mou T'ai River and fireworks.

Sylvia and I tossed the burning liquid back like western cowboys. Our noses reddened and tears sprang to our eyes. Chou looked on with concern and amusement. "If you like, you can try our red wine," he said. "It is not so strong."

Premier Chou looked relaxed, extremely handsome and much younger than his seventy-three years. A beautiful girl in her early twenties with long braids brought in a steaming dish of baby shrimps with king crab meat and Chou said it was from the province of Hupei. Then he introduced Dad to the girl, who was also from Hupei. Chou was delighted when Dad talked to her in her native dialect. He threw his head back and laughed like a little boy who had sprung a pleasant surprise.

Dad and the Premier began to talk about their home towns, which happen to be in neighboring provinces, and before long they were exchanging old Chinese jokes and riddles. The riddles are asked in a rhyming, almost sing-song Chinese, and when Dad asks them he sounds like an old Chinese opera singer, which is much funnier than the riddle itself. Ch'iao Kuan-hua, the vice-foreign minister, a tall, charming man Dad has known for years, laughed so hard I began to worry. In English the riddles lose their wit, but here is an example of one Dad asked: "What is a golden ax with a silver handle?"

Everyone pondered and repeated the riddle. The Premier of China assumed a look of mock concern as if he were solving a great world problem. He conferred with his top advisers and darted glances at the big gray-haired foreigner who sat grinning across the table.

Then they gave up. "What is it?" asked Chou.

"A bean sprout!" roared Dad, filling the room with fiendish laughter.

"Now here's another," he said gleefully, and sang out: "There was an old man of eighty-eight whose whiskers grew in before his teeth. What is it?"

More pondering. This was a very

Several delicious courses followed and talk became more serious. Chou En-lai explained the development of the Sino-Soviet ideological split in intriguing detail while we enthusiastically consumed sugar pea shoots with elephants' ears (black wood fungus), hot bamboo tipped in chicken fat, steamed rice sticks stuffed with gingered meat and a dish called Lion's Head in Amber Sauce which looked suspiciously like my homemade meat balls and gravy but did not taste like it.

We raved so much about the Eight Heavenly Flavors dessert that the Premier had the cook write out the ingredients and explain how to make it: It is really quite simple; just take dates, sweet plums, peaches, raisins, gherkins—rinds and seeds—lotus seeds, ginger and red beans. Chop them all up and pour in a mold with rice and sweet water. Let it steam until the rice is soft. Cool. Turn over, pour on syrup, sprinkle with sesame seeds and *voilà!* Eight Heavenly Flavors is yours.

After dinner the Premier graciously conceded to Sylvia's and my bourgeois request that he autograph our menus. Later he took Dad to see the Hupei Room, having recalled where it was situated, and presented him with pictures of it—to remember, he said, this evening with an old friend. Then Chou wished Dad good luck and fair weather for his journey back home to Hupei.

serious question. Finally Huang Hua looked triumphant.

"Corn on the cob!" he said victoriously.

"Right," said Dad. "Good for you!" But he looked disappointed. Meanwhile something was brewing in Chou En-lai's corner.

"All right now," Chou said, looking like Charlie Chan. "I'll give you one: What is green and red and lies between two slabs of white jade?"

The more Dad puzzled, the brighter Chou became. Sylvia tried to come to Dad's rescue.

"A lettuce and tomato sandwich," she volunteered.

Chou shook his head and laughed.

"No!" he said, looking pleased as Punch. "It's a stuffed bun."

We raised our glasses in a *kan-pei* (bottoms up) to the winners.

Journey
to the Past 遊历亦戌

[46]

RETURN HOME TO FANCHENG

Chester A. Ronning

In May 1971, accompanied by my daughters Sylvia and Audrey, I returned to visit my home town in the interior of China. It was a moving experience, after forty-four years, to return to Fancheng to visit the old haunts and to see some of the friends I had known since childhood days.

I was born in Fancheng of missionary parents in 1894 and brought up there until I was nearly thirteen. I returned to teach school from 1922 to 1927.

Fancheng has been for millennia a flourishing commercial twin city of Siangyang in Hupei province. These two walled cities, one on each side of the Han River, are known as Siangfan.

Siangfan was famous in Chinese history, for it was here that Chu-ko Liang, one of China's greatest heroes, who came from Shantung, received the training and education which prepared him to become prime minister of one of China's ancient kingdoms.

When I was a boy in Fancheng, we could look up and across the Han River from our upstairs veranda to see in the distance, resting on the south bank, a mountain which resembled a majestic, heavily maned lion. In the forest of ancient trees on the mountain lion's

[47]

[48]

head there was an old temple which had been maintained for centuries, dedicated to the memory of Chu-ko Liang. Within the temple courtyards, magnificent *mu-tan hua*, shrub peonies, ancient China's national flower, were carefully nurtured.

In the old days scholars from Siang-fan—Siangyang and Fancheng—and their families made annual pilgrimages to the temple when the *mu-tan hua* were in full bloom.

As a boy, and years later as a teacher in Fancheng, I had frequently visited this charming sylvan retreat in the dense forests. Today the park is carefully preserved and is visited by thousands of workers, peasants and students, brought by buses to enjoy the atmosphere of ancient China during vacations from the duties of farm, factory or school.

On this trip we traveled from Wuhan to Fancheng by train. Sylvia and Audrey were disappointed because they had hoped to travel as we had in the old days, sailing leisurely up the Han in a comfortable houseboat. It usually took a month to make the journey of almost six hundred miles, as the river winds in numerous S-turns. My daughters' hopes were frustrated by modern transportation and we sped across the country only two hundred miles as the crow flies in an air-conditioned railway coach taking only eight hours.

The country was hilly and green. Low rolling mountains were always visible in the distance. Lush weeping willows hung low over the streams. Women were beating their clothes clean on flat rocks. I had been through this country during the warlord days in the 1920s when it was inhabited by roving bandits and disbanded troops who terrorized the inhabitants. In those days the villages were clusters of mud huts with straw roofs. They were surrounded by high mud walls for protection and each had a watchtower with a sentry keeping constant vigilance for robbers. Now the walls and watchtowers are gone and the mud huts have been replaced by brick houses with tile roofs. Bricks are shaped from the local red clay and baked in homemade kilns.

Approaching Fancheng, we could see the Pien Shan, the mountains where we used to spend our summer vacations. In the old days the mountains were naked. The trees had been cut down and even the roots were dug up for fuel. Today the mountains have been reforested. When I saw the transformed appearance of the countryside, and the wide expanses of fields of rice, wheat, barley, soy beans and vegetables, it was sometimes difficult to remember that one was actually in China.

The city of Fancheng had also changed nearly beyond recognition in

many respects. The city walls had come
down on all sides, except on the river
front. Only the old moat is now visible.
The city had expanded far beyond the
old walls, especially to the northeast.

We were met at the railway station
by a welcoming committee. There were
also hundreds of residents and some of
my old friends who had come to see
the first foreigners to visit their city in
over twenty years. They had read about
our anticipated visit in the local press.
When I greeted them, speaking Chinese
with a strong Siangyang accent which
I had acquired as a child, they re-
sponded with warm greetings and
welcoming smiles.

Automobiles, made in China, con-
veyed us through the industrial part of
the city, outside of where the walls had
been. We crossed the ancient moat
around the old city to the modern new
bridge which spans the Han River. On
the Siangyang side, the city walls of the
old official city still stand. The moats,
which were lined with beautiful willows, are the widest I have seen around
any walled city in China. We drove
through the East Gate to a comfortable
rest house where special preparations
had been made for our stay.

I had warned my daughters that unless they were prepared to take it on the
chin—if that is where you take it when
sleeping on the hard boards in an old-
fashioned Chinese inn—they should

not come with me to Siangfan. Their reply was that they could do anything I could, but better. To my astonishment, we had not only soft, comfortable beds but hot and cold running water, modern bathtubs and flush toilets. The rooms were quaintly furnished with bamboo furniture, blue cotton curtains and double beds with hand-embroidered satin quilts and pillowcases.

Shortly after arriving we were treated to a multicourse Western-style breakfast, and then, with some of the residents of Siangyang accompanying us, we went sightseeing. We climbed the drum-and-bell tower and walked along the city wall where I had walked with my father in the 1890s and with Sylvia in the 1920s. From the wall we looked across the river to the Lutheran mission compound where I was born.

Later we crossed the river back to Fancheng to visit the compound. The old church, which was built under my father's supervision, still stands in perfect condition. It is not used for services, but I was told by a friend from the old days that a group of aged Christians still meet periodically in the guest room of the church. The old gray-and-red structure was still beautifully reflected in the clear water of the pond where I played as a child.

The original school building had been replaced by a much larger, new building, which we visited. The principal

welcomed us warmly and reminded my daughters that Halvor Ronning had established the first modern school here, which was opened on August 4, 1894. My father had told me that he had visited numerous families in the area and tried to persuade them to send their children to school. But on the first day, when he came to the little schoolhouse, he found only one ragged urchin sitting on the steps. But Father never gave up. The next day there were two pupils and on the third day there were five. For the old missionaries that was called progress. By the time he left in 1908, he had about fifty students. When I returned in 1922 to teach at the middle school (high school), there were two hundred students in addition to the same number of primary school students. The enrollment today is 1,327 students.

We also looked in on the girls' school founded by my mother, Hannah Rorem Ronning. When she died in 1907, the school had only about thirty students. It has also expanded into thousands. My mother was buried in the compound and her tombstone still stands near the school grounds. She would have been gratified to see the well-dressed, well-fed children of the school she started, playing games, singing, dancing and romping around the spacious grounds during the extended (for our benefit) forenoon recess.

On another day we traveled west of Siangyang to visit a rural commune. There I saw former swampland, where there had been only weeds and frogs, transformed into fertile green fields in which two crops of rice are produced annually instead of one, and each crop produces three times the yield of earlier days. Agriculture is not yet mechanized in my home district, and one still sees the peasants plowing the fields with their long-horned water buffalo as they have for centuries. But scientific selection of the best seed, chemical fertilizer and new techniques have enabled the farmers to produce enough food for all. They also grow sufficient cotton to clothe everyone, as well as for export to other areas of China.

I was particularly impressed by the cotton textile factory outside the city limits of old Fancheng. For the first time in my life I was moved by machinery when I saw hundreds of automatic looms driven by electric power and attended by only a few girls dressed in white. Tons of white cloth came out of the machines to be packed into bales to clothe the peasants. In the old days most of the people had been inadequately clothed, a large percentage in tattered rags. During this visit to China I did not see a single person in Siangfan, or for that matter in any other part of China, who suffered from lack of clothing. In the communes there was more white clothing than any other color for the simple reason that white unprinted cloth is cheaper. The inhabitants of the rural communes, where most of the people of China live, are by no means all dressed in drab gray and blue clothing.

At the factory, where most of the employees were young people, we were entertained in a spacious hall by ballet dancers, a mixed chorus and an orchestra, all the members of which were local factory workers. The performances were almost of professional quality.

I also noted that the textile factory in Fancheng was more modern in some respects than the older textile factories we saw in Peking. They had, for

example, suction vents to clear the lint from the air and the noise level was much lower. The policy of China today is to diversify industry throughout the country. Factories are under construction in all formerly unindustrialized areas.

Before the People's Republic came into power there was almost no modern industry in the Fancheng area. Here there had been only one machine repair shop with twenty-one workers, four handicraft shops, a cigarette-rolling shop and about one hundred blacksmiths. Mr. Ho Ping-wu, vice-chairman of the Revolutionary Committee, informed us that there are now over two hundred big and small factories with a total value of 117 million yuan, and over three hundred retail stores. We visited the main department store and found a wide variety of consumer goods of all types.

Mr. Ho also said they now had fourteen hospitals and clinics in the city and 1,900 medical workers, compared to three hospitals and six hundred medical workers before the Revolution. When I asked about the average income, he said it was comparatively low because the new factories brought in many new workers with lower salaries. In 1965 the average wage was 800 yuan per year, but it had now dropped to 600 and 700 yuan a year. Mr. Ho, like many of the other Chinese workers and

[55]

officials I talked to, pointed out short-comings and said there was still a long way to go. There is no unemployment, and I was informed that they could use more manpower. Mr. Ho said: "We must raise our standard of mechanization in agriculture and raise our potential to fight natural catastrophes." He added that last year the cotton yield had dropped and there were still many unpaved roads.

I agreed that there was much to be accomplished but I got the impression that there was constant improvement. When I was a child here, many of the people did not have a roof over their heads. Only rich merchants, officials and landlords had adequate housing. Now everyone has a home. They are not big or elaborate, but they are adequate and clean, and the people are proud of them.

In Fancheng I learned that the people of my home town were certainly not the faceless, regimented robots some foreigners have reported the people of China to be. They are enthusiastic not only about their participation in the labor in the factories and communes, but about their opportunities to participate in social activities and in theater, music, dancing and the arts.

I learned this through conversations with former friends, some of whom had been virtually brought up in my home in Fancheng. The son of one of

my mother's best friends, Li San-chieh, for example, came to welcome me. Although he was nearly my age, he had been my student. When I was his teacher, he was an enthusiastic revolutionary. Now he was enthusiastic about the accomplishments of the Revolution and especially about the Cultural Revolution. Another of my students, who was four years older than I, came with his son and daughter-in-law to visit us. We spoke only in Chinese, but when I introduced him to my daughters, he spoke to them in excellent idiomatic English which he had learned years ago and still remembered.

After we had reminisced about the old days and caught up on the activities of mutual friends, he proudly informed me that he and his wife had helped to build the bridge over the Han River. When I interjected that I had no idea that he was a civil engineer, he said,

"Oh, no, we only helped to move earth together with other volunteer workers to build the approaches to the bridge. You came over our bridge in the automobile, did you not? Well, if we had not built the approaches, you could have got neither on nor off the bridge. My wife and I helped with shovels and wheelbarrows."

I never thought in the old days that I would ever hear an intellectual say that he was proud of having used his hands to move dirt.

I was very impressed by the attitudes and reactions revealed to me by old acquaintances concerning what had happened during the past twenty years, since the People's Republic of China had come to power. There was no doubt about the material progress that had been achieved, which had raised the standard of living in food, clothing and shelter to higher levels than I had thought possible in two decades. I wanted to learn from them, however, how they felt about whatever it had cost them to attain the relatively higher standards that were so evident. From conversations with them and their sons and daughters, I realized that a new spirit had replaced the old servile attitude to their superiors. Today they are enthusiastic about their participation, not only in activities but also in decision-making. I could not help but think that my

missionary parents would have been most pleased to note how the people of Fancheng have been liberated from the old superstitions and from the crippling limitations of the past.

Chester A. Ronning

SAILING THE HAN

In Fancheng we sailed the Han in a
pien tsu. Dad and his Chinese friends
went to great pains to find exactly the
same type of freight junk he had last
sailed in forty-four years earlier to
Hankow. In the days of my grandparents, the trip from Hankow was
made in *mankans*, comfortable passenger houseboats.

About an hour downriver, we fell in
with a picturesque fleet of freight junks
with their patched, bamboo-ribbed
sails, full-blown in the wind. Most were
carrying coal, while others carried
cargoes of stone and marble from the
quarries. When the fleet got into the
lee of a bend, it was forced to stop, and
to our delight we had the chance to
witness a scene from centuries past.
All the sailors except two in each boat
jumped out and waded ashore with
cables and harnesses to prepare to pull
the vessels upriver.

The boat in front of us was a one-
family enterprise. The mother steered
the rudder while the father stood in
the bow holding a long bamboo pole
with a metal point called a *kao*. He
used this to prevent the boat from
beaching or colliding with the others.
Their two grown children, a boy and a
girl, took their harnesses and the cable
and climbed up the riverbank to a path
running parallel to the water. The

cable, made of bamboo, was attached to the top of the mast so it could be tossed over the mast of any passing boat if necessary. The other end was attached with a silk rope through a wooden peg and then bound to the canvas shoulder harness. The peg enables the puller to loosen the harness if the junk should slide backward. Several harnesses can be attached to the same cable. We waded ashore and ran up the path to watch the pullers. In a few minutes their harnesses were attached and they were straining against the swiftly flowing current, with mother and the other captains shouting clipped orders. With every muscle taut, grunting in unison and lying almost flat against the harness, they got the boats moving upstream. The girl, momentarily diverted by our cameras, lost her step and her family's boat began to slide back. Dad grabbed for the cable and pulled until it was safely back on course. Captain Mother was furious and from the stern she spewed curses into the air. This was a river they loved and feared and they never played with it.

When the wind picked up, we sailed leisurely back to Fancheng and Dad told Sylvia and me about the Yangtze Gorges, where it sometimes took a hundred men to pull a junk through the raging current.

We also talked about his parents,

[61]

Halvor and Hannah Ronning, who in May 1894, exactly seventy-seven years earlier, had been stranded for two days on the same Han River. But theirs was not a sentimental journey like ours. They were going to Fancheng from Hankow to establish the first Lutheran mission in the area. With them were two children, their own two-year-old son Nelius and a ten-year-old Chinese boy named Wang Tang, the son of a pagan warlord who had implored them to bring Wang up as a Christian. They had later adopted the boy and loved him as their own. On the river trip Wang fell overboard and drowned. Grandfather wrote in his diary: "On the 9th day of May, 1894 we had the dreadful misfortune that our dear son, Wang Tang, drowned. It was a stunning blow! I had great expectations for him, perhaps too great. . . ."

A few days later they were stranded and Grandfather recorded:

May 17, 1894—We had great excitement yesterday. We had to remain here two days on account of lack of wind. When the people in the surrounding country heard that foreigners were on board, they came in great crowds to look at us. In the afternoon the wind had risen and our men began to pull the boat. Now things began to happen. An eight-year-old boy had disappeared, and the father and mother came to our boat and claimed that we had stolen the boy. The crowd grew furious and stopped the boat and wanted to come on board and search for the boy.

We were struck with fear, because almost all riots begin with wild rumors which people believe. The parents kept on crying aloud. The situation became tense. We cried to the Almighty for help. We suggested that two men might come on board and see. This they would not or dared not do; all of them wanted to come. Our captain made a speech saying that he was Chinese and had with him twenty other Chinese who could testify that we had not stolen the boy. Fortunately, we heard that the local mandarin lived nearby. We sent a messenger to him. He came and the larger part of the people went home. God be praised! Soon they all left and we had a peaceful night. Today we have heard nothing more about the boy. Either someone had concocted a lie or the boy had run away from home or fallen into the river.

Although the junks remain the same as they were during the days of my grandparents, the mighty Han River they sailed on has been contained by higher dikes.

Dad recalled how the people here used to live in terror of the Han. "When I was a boy in these parts," he said, "the Chinese peasants firmly believed that an angry dragon descended from the sky and plunged into the Han River, causing the waters to rise up and flood the countryside, villages and sometimes whole cities. Illiterate people fatalistically accepted the inevitability of periodic floods."

Formerly if the river rose very much over the normal water level, the whole area was flooded. In 1938 over three thousand people were drowned. The last flood was in 1964. After that the people took fate into their own hands and strengthened the dikes along both sides of the Han. The river can now rise far above the normal level without flooding. Gates in the dikes are also constructed to provide irrigation water during drought periods.

Our visit to Fancheng had not taken long, but it took me back a century.

Chinese
Life Styles

中国生活方式

[64]

CHANGING CITIES

The most striking change for visitors who have seen Chinese cities before the Revolution is that they have been cleaned up—physically and morally There is no organized crime, no filth, no beggars and little night life.

Shanghai is China's largest city. Over six million people live in the old inner city and four million more live in the surrounding suburbs. The business district was owned mostly by foreign concessions during the days of Western imperialism. But now the Hong Kong Shanghai Bank, which was once the citadel of British finance in China, is the headquarters of the Shanghai Revolutionary Committee, and the clock tower, which once chimed like London's Big Ben, now rings out a tune from "The East Is Red."

Soochow Creek, which once reeked with hideous odors, has been dredged. The ramshackle slums have been replaced with apartment buildings and trees have been planted.

It has long since been taken for granted that the standard of living has been raised in the cities of China, and that the streets are clean, but to walk the streets of Shanghai, which was once considered the wickedest port in the East, at midnight without fear of being robbed is even more surprising than the lack of the night people, cars, jazzy nightclubs, superrich and superpoor, mah-jongg clacks, prostitutes, opium addicts and gambling dens that made up old Shanghai.

The Bund, or Shanghai waterfront, was once a hangout for foreign sailors, smugglers and adventurers. Now the glittering signs have been replaced by propaganda posters and portraits of Mao Tse-tung and the waterfront has become a favorite place for evening strollers and morning exercises.

Life might seem dull to a Western visitor or a Scandinavian sailor, but the Chinese no longer care what foreigners find dull or exciting. The cities belong to China once again and they are free from exploiters and big-city crime.

The Chinese have fought crime with the same vigorous, politically oriented enthusiasm with which they fought hunger. Shortly after the Revolution, drug addicts were all sent to rehabilitation centers, and gambling dens and houses of prostitution were closed in a mass clean-up move. Since then, the crime rate has remained low because the people will no longer tolerate it. The Maoist ideology strongly condemns crime as detrimental to the state as a whole, and therefore the potential sinner is confronted not only with a possible prison term if caught but with the disdain of his friends if he is successful. Second, with no organized criminal underground, there is no place to sell stolen wares, no place to escape.

But among almost 800 million people there is, of course, still some crime and China still has its prisons. A petty offender is first given a strong lecture by the police on his moral obligations toward his fellow human beings, the state, and the philosophy of Mao Tse-tung. This is often supported by pressure from the offender's peers and neighbors. If he repents and vows to mend his ways, he is set free, but if he repeats the crime, he is tried in a People's Court and, if found guilty, sentenced to prison.

The Chinese attempt to rehabilitate their lawbreakers to become useful members of society. In Nanking we visited a prison and were shown through the wards, mess halls, workrooms and the classrooms where they spend hours of study. The prison commissioner said the Chinese do not believe that if a man commits a crime his attitude can be changed by merely locking him up for a few years. They feel that the criminal's thinking and his whole approach to life should be changed. This is done not through physical punishment but through political education and labor. On the question of returnees, the warden said:

"Occasionally a former prisoner comes back, but this is rare. The government gives them jobs and they enjoy equal rights. There is no looking down on them, because their ideology has become good and they don't think about crime."

In the prison courtyard stood two guards with bayoneted rifles. These were the first armed guards I had seen in the prison. When I remarked on this, the warden replied, "We don't need many guards."

"But what if a prisoner tries to escape?" I asked.

"Escape!" he answered. "Where would he escape to? If his ideology is not good, the people will turn him in again. There is no place to escape to."

It took a while to comprehend the significance of his answer, but I knew there was a lot of truth in it because the government is so organized that it can exert political and ideological control. This control is not exerted by command. China is not a police state. There are no armed police visible apart from traffic police and no soldiers patrol the streets. The methods used by the government to win the participation of the people are constant propaganda, persuasion and education.

The means of exerting this type of control require complex administration, but the idea is basically a simple one. It is made possible by organizing the people of China into small work units of twenty to thirty people; in the cities they are called neighborhood committees, which are responsible to larger units called street committees, and in the communes they are production teams, which are responsible to brigades. These represent the grass roots of society and are where the people solve their day-to-day problems. Each unit is supervised by a Revolutionary Committee with representatives from the party, the army and the workers. Their duty is to encourage all members to participate in political activities, and all activities in China are political. They organize political study classes, where attendance is recorded. The group reads the philosophy of Mao and discusses ways to improve their production and living standards. If a member slackens in his duties, he is criticized until he acknowledges the error of his ways or, as a member of a Shanghai neighborhood committee said, "If there are any differences of opinion, we mediate until all the good neighbors are united as one."

The street committees exercise a strong moral force over the people in their area, and when this power is directed toward rehabilitating a former criminal, the offender will think twice before repeating the offense.

City Living

Five- and six-story apartment buildings are being built in the cities to replace the old houses, and in the suburbs to house workers in factory complexes. The apartments usually have two rooms, with tables, beds, chests, wardrobes and radios. There are separate kitchens, bathrooms, and small balconies where they dry the clothes. Each housing development has its own marketplace, and a large canteen where workers can buy meals if they wish. The canteen kitchens are modern and clean, with large white tile stoves heated by gas or coal. Meals are cheap. The canteens are popular for lunch but most evening meals are taken at home. Frozen foods are not available, but fresh food already chopped and seasoned for cooking can be purchased.

There are no dishwashers or other modern appliances except sewing machines, which are very popular, and a few clothes-washing machines. The cities have inexpensive laundries, but in the country the clothes are mostly washed by hand in the local stream, where the ladies get together to gossip and washday becomes a social affair. The clothes are cleaned without the aid of detergents or bleach, dried in the sun on bamboo poles, and rarely ironed.

Each city has its own kind of hous-

ing. In Peking a typical old residence, for those not in apartments, is built of gray brick with a gray tile roof. It encloses a square courtyard, with a gate facing south. The courtyard is the center of activity for the various families. Here the children play and study and the families do much of the cooking, sharing the common water tap. The main wing of the house, which is on the far side of the courtyard, also faces south to catch the sun. This type of house is called *ssu-ho yuan.* Pagoda trees usually stand in front of the gate, while date and fruit trees grow in the courtyard.

Visitors who lived in China before the Revolution are struck by the abundance of food in China today. Large poultry, meat and vegetable markets are conveniently located near every housing and factory unit in the cities and in the villages on the communes. Prices are stable and almost the same throughout China. The average shopper buys for one day at a time because refrigerators are rare. The Chinese always carry their own baskets or string bags to the marketplace, so there is no waste paper.

Shopping

Compared to America and other Western countries, the supply and variety of consumer goods in Chinese department stores are rather limited, but the stores are stacked with a wide range of useful and colorful goods for every type of Chinese consumer, and for a Westerner, who finds even everyday Chinese things new and interesting, the stores are a delightful source of exploration and discovery.

One finds things like lacquer bowls, acupuncture needles, ivory chopsticks, calligraphy brushes, painted fans, Red Army knapsacks and belts, unfamiliar musical instruments, wooden abacuses, teacups with tops and tons of other exciting things that are just ordinary to the Chinese.

In the department stores, the largest sections are usually those selling yard goods and jackets. Other departments offer radios and cameras, records and musical instruments; furs from Mongolia and Tibet; groceries of all kinds, including a wide selection of wines, Chinese liquors and whiskeys; books and posters; and cosmetics, for which one brings empty containers to be refilled.

The most colorful section is the toy department, where adults as well as children gather to watch the mechanical toys. The center of attraction in a Peking store when we were shopping was a fat tin hen laying eggs as she pecked around a counter. Also enticing is the bedding section, where bright satin quilts and pillowcases, hand embroidered with birds and flowers, are displayed.

The basic goods, like ordinary material for clothing, and shoes, bedding, kitchen utensils, bicycles and radios, are pretty much the same everywhere in China, and so are the prices, because all stores are state-owned. We saw the same things for the same price in Peking, Shenyang, Hankow and Canton.

Prices seem low, but compared to the low wage structure of the economy they are rather high. A quilt, for instance, is around $2.50 and a pillowcase eighty cents; a child's suit about two dollars or less, and hat about sixty cents. Shoes range from one dollar for canvas to five dollars for leather. A man or woman's cotton suit averages about six dollars, blouses and men's shirts about two dollars, padded jackets from four to six dollars depending on the material.

The industrial worker makes between fourteen and forty-five dollars per month, while higher salaries in other brackets range up to about $140 per month. No taxes are taken out of this. Electricity costs about forty cents per month, rent around three dollars and food from three to four dollars

a person per month when one eats at home. Medical expenses are usually free for all workers, but dependents pay about nine cents per year, although this varies according to the area. This leaves very little money per month for the average worker to spend on clothing and luxuries such as entertainment, radios, et cetera. A bicycle costs about fifty dollars, so it would take a few months' savings. There are no installment plans. Nevertheless, the stores are always full of people buying all sorts of things, always in a relaxed, good-humored way. Shoppers spend a long time discussing the pros and cons of an item with the attendants before purchasing. The attendants are polite and are trained to help the inexperienced shopper make the right decision, especially in the pharmaceutical department.

Articles can of course be returned if not satisfactory and repairs are made in the shops. A small section of the department stores with essential goods and medicines remains open for workers on night shifts.

Besides the department stores there are small shops specializing in old and new scrolls, painted fans, modern handicrafts, books and posters, reproductions of ancient sculpture and stone rubbings, old jewelry and carvings in jade and semiprecious stones, wicker furniture, luggage and bedding, among other things.

[73]

The Chinese in the cities rise almost as early as those in the country—usually around 6:00 A.M. in the summer and 7:00 A.M. in midwinter—and they turn in around 10:30 P.M., although some restaurants are open until 11:00 P.M.

The Chinese stress physical fitness, and in the early morning hours, children, women and men of all ages can be seen exercising. Some march, jog, or kick high, but the favorite exercise, especially for the elderly, is T'ai Ch'i Ch'uan, that ancient art of posturing, deliberate movement and rhythms, which foreigners sometimes call shadowboxing. T'ai Ch'i Ch'uan, more than just an exercise, is a formal discipline that requires intense concentration and control of mind and body. Executed correctly, it imparts a sense of well-being and inner tranquillity to the performer.

Work begins at 8:00 or 9:00 A.M. and an average industrial worker living in a city works seven and a half hours a day, six days a week, with fifteen-minute tea breaks in the morning and afternoon and a nap after lunch. This custom is common throughout China, and from the noon hour until two-thirty or three o'clock in the summer, the cities are blissfully quiet. The regular workday is over at 6:30 P.M., but many factories have night shifts. The

[75]

new factories are being built on the outskirts of the cities, but there are still some factories in heavy industrial cities like Shanghai, and in Shenyang and Anshan in the northeast.

In Shanghai many of the factories are located along the banks of the Whangpoo River, which empties into the harbor. The air of the waterfront is polluted by the black smoke pouring out of the chimneys. Shanghai has the largest industrial output of any city in China. Among other things it produces textiles, trucks and the Red Flag cars used by government officials. The people of Shanghai also make machinery, electronic equipment, turbines, chemicals and over two million tons of steel a year.

In China married couples often work in the same factory or factory complex. Housing, schools, hospitals, restaurants, shops and recreational facilities are also available in the area. After work the couples pick up their small children from day care centers and go home or to a community dining hall for dinner. Like everywhere else, it is cheaper but more work to eat at home. The working couple lucky enough to have an older member of the family to help with the children and housework usually eat at home. Occasionally they will also go to one of the many restaurants or *hsiao-ch'ih tien* (wine rooms) available in every Chinese city.

[77]

Going Out

A night on the town usually means going to a local theater to see a revolutionary drama and then to a little wine room for a beer and a snack. There are several "modern revolutionary dramas" and new ones are always in production. These presentations consist of operas, ballets and concerts with names like "Taking Tiger Mountain by Strategy," "The White-Haired Girl" and "The Red Lantern." When we were there, the most popular one seemed to be "Red Detachment of Women," which is a ballet starring a troop of lovely and patriotic girls in shorts.

Most of the dramas depict the struggles of oppressed peasants against cruel landlords, corrupt Nationalist officials and hissing Japanese generals, who are constantly being outwitted and physically overthrown by beautiful girls with pure revolutionary hearts. The drama is intense, the battle scenes (often bordering on slapstick) are fierce, the music is fast and loud, the dancing superb, and the acrobatics incredible. There is always a hopeful if not happy ending because even if the hero is killed, his cause is carried forward by other self-sacrificing supporters. The theaters, which mostly have simple decor with hard seats, are usually jammed with workers and young people, who obviously enjoy the performances and participate by clapping for the heroes and laughing at the villains, who besides being wicked are also stupid fools. The rousing revolutionary music is punctuated with the zings and gongs of old Chinese opera just as their modern ballet is combined with stylized stances, exaggerated facial expressions and double takes.

Modern costumes are accentuated by the old-style makeup evoking well-known opera characteristics. The hero, for example, has a rosy face, while the cowardly villain is greenish. A crafty villain has elongated slit eyes, and the warrior is painted in blacks and whites, showing his valor and hot temper. Like every other aspect of Chinese society today, the performing arts are politically motivated. One of the aims of the Cultural Revolution in the field of the dramatic arts is to bring theater back to the masses and through this medium educate them to the importance of keeping the spirit of the Revolution alive.

Films are also shown regularly in cinemas in the cities and the communes. In the cities, Saturday nights are the busiest for cinemas, a common form of after-dinner entertainment. Their "cowboys and Indians" are the revolutionaries and counterrevolutionaries or the peasants and the landlords. The themes are black and white, but the photography is often in color and sometimes very artistic. There are no scenes of sex, sadistic violence or crime, which are considered to be not only in very bad taste but signs of a decadent society.

Live theater is preferred to movies, and every organized unit in China has regular shows put on by rotating amateur members of the group. They often make up plays about their everyday lives. In Fancheng, for instance, workers in a cotton textile mill gave a skit about their jobs. Tots in a nursery in Shanghai waved homemade flowers and sang about carrying on the Revolution.

The traditional lion dance has been a favorite entertainment for the Chinese for centuries. It has recently been revived by the Shenyang Acrobatic Troupe, a company of fifty-five extraordinary acrobats, magicians and musicians, who became the first entertainers from the People's Republic to tour Canada and the United States. On special occasions, like May Day, outdoor theaters are set up in the gardens and parks. Here some soldiers of the People's Liberation Army give a concert near a palace in the Forbidden City of Peking.

All of the performances we saw were executed with remarkable confidence and great gusto, and after the show was over the audience left the theater in a gay mood, with many of them singing or whistling snatches of songs from the performance.

Those wanting to make a night of it can go on to one of the many large or small restaurants. The restaurants specialize in dishes from Canton, Szechwan, Peking, Mongolia, Shanghai and other areas famous for their food. There are three restaurants in Peking that serve only Peking duck. The prices range from three to six yuan, depending on the number of courses. For three yuan ($1.23) one gets several courses plus beer and mou-t'ai. For six yuan ($2.46) one gets a fantastic feast. There are also Japanese and Western-style restaurants, but the ordinary people usually go to the small cafés, where one can order local wine or beer for about ten cents a pint with a side dish of chicken or shrimp in black bean sauce, or a spring roll for about four cents. A bowl of won-ton soup costs about seven cents. Another favorite gathering and gossiping place is around the open food stalls, where vendors dish out aromatic bowls of hot rice and noodles with delicious prawns and spiced meat balls.

Although the people like to enjoy themselves and one hears much laughter in the restaurants, they seldom overindulge or drink too much.

On weekends and holidays people from the communes come by truck, train and bicycle to enjoy the restaurants, sample the wines, go shopping and join the city dwellers in the already overcrowded streets.

Holidays

Sundays and holidays in China are much like Sundays and holidays everywhere else. Families and friends get together to go sightseeing, boating, visiting, picnicking, and to see sports events.

One Sunday Dad, Sylvia and I joined the people in East Lake Park on the outskirts of Wuchang, which lies opposite Hankow on the Yangtze River. We had been touring in an open motorboat, but our trip was cut short by pouring rain and we retreated to the shelter of a large restaurant sprawled on the banks of the lake. Young people who had also moved in from the wet gardens sat around the tables drinking tea and playing cards and dominoes. A small shop was selling nuts, fruits, chocolates and a variety of wines and liquors, and, as if to set the mood, a sign in English and Chinese over the wine display advised: "Heartily Wish Chairman Mao a Long Long Life."

After the rain the edges of the lake soon filled with people swimming, rowing and fishing, and in the gardens people of all ages squatted in circles or sat around tables playing checkers and go. The children were in the fields playing soccer and football games while others ran various kinds of races. In the background stood a large red billboard containing a poem by Mao

[86]

written in white characters of his own calligraphy.

Some of the young people played Ping-Pong in the open pavilions. Table tennis is obviously the most popular sport, and one sees makeshift tables set up in school playgrounds, hotel patios and workers' settlements. The Chinese also like fencing, basketball and track and field. There are indoor and outdoor stadiums or playing fields in every city and commune. The Peking Capital Stadium, for instance, holds 100,000 people and usually plays to a full house. The State Sports Commission sets the rules and standards and supervises the various competitive sports. China does not compete in the Olympics but takes part in other international events throughout Asia and parts of Europe.

In Nanking, Chiang Kai-shek's old capital, a favorite place for Sunday outings is Sun Yat-sen's Tomb and the

surrounding parks on the southern slopes of Purple Mountain. Dad, Sylvia and I spent a Sunday afternoon wandering around the gardens and visiting a nearby pagoda built by the Nationalists and called Murphy's Pagoda by the foreigners. Then we climbed the hundreds of steps to visit the crypt where Sun Yat-sen's body has been lying in a marble casket since 1929 and from where one gets a stupendous view of the surrounding countryside. At first I thought the mausoleum was about the only thing in Nanking that had not changed since we lived there before the Revolution, but on closer inspection I noticed that two mosaic blue-and-white flags of the Kuomintang that had decorated the ceiling above statues of Sun Yat-sen, which I had seen in 1966, had been torn out during the Cultural Revolution. As yet nothing had replaced them, but I suspect on my next trip red flags will be embedded over the head of the man often called the "Father of the Revolution" by both the Nationalists and the Communists.

Unfortunately, rain and fog obstructed the view of Nanking, but in my mind's eye I saw a hundred scenes from the "old days" when China was in the throes of a revolution that was to change it forever.

Sundays in Shenyang find the people relaxing on the graves of their former emperors. The historic Ch'ing Tombs

on the outskirts of Shenyang are a favorite place for the northeasterners to picnic in the gardens, go boating in the lake, stroll along the walls or explore the ancient towers.

The cities, with their 140 million people, have long since spilled over their ancient walls into sprawling suburbs. There is a move to leave the cities and establish small, self-sufficient towns called "satellites" with their own agriculture and industry.

Strangely enough, in this heavily populated land there are still uninhabited areas, rich in natural resources, in the northern and northwestern regions. The young people especially are encouraged to leave the cities and, like the pioneers of the American West, develop virgin lands. In the last five years, over twenty million have moved out of the cities in a program dubbed "Head for the Country."

[89]

LIFE ON A CHINESE COMMUNE

In the past Chinese peasants, because of the feudal system, had little hope of raising their living standard above bare survival. They were plagued with famine, disease, poverty and illiteracy.

As the Communists took control of the mainland they carried out a land reform program. Land was distributed equally among the peasants. Landlords who were charged with crimes against tenants were submitted to People's Courts. Unknown thousands were condemned to death, while others were given a chance to reform through labor. The land was first merged into cooperatives. Later, during the Great Leap Forward in 1958, it was collectivized and people's farm communes were formed.

Each commune is a microcosm of the transformed rural society of Communist China. It functions as a largely self-supporting community engaged in some form of agriculture with supporting trades such as handicrafts and light industries. There are also printing and broadcasting facilities. Ninety percent of rural China consists of communes, which may vary in size from about ten thousand to sixty thousand people. Communes are composed of brigades, which are made up of production teams. Each production team consists of about two dozen families, who are responsible for their own productivity. About fifteen teams or about 450 families (which could mean several villages) make up one brigade. From ten to thirty brigades make a commune.

Since the Cultural Revolution of 1966–1969, the communes have been directed by Revolutionary Committees, which were established at every administrative level. The committee members are representatives of the three major sections of Chinese society: cadres (members of the party or government), soldiers and veteran peasant workers.

Although all communes are basically run in the same way, they are visually very different, depending on the geography and what they produce.

One of the communes I visited during my ten weeks in China was in the dry hills near Sian. The commune consisted of eleven brigades. I went to the Shuang Wang brigade, which is on 2,750 mou of land (about 420 acres) made up of five villages, seven production teams, 356 households and 1,812 members. Director Liu Shu-chen, a man with a strong weather-beaten face and shaven head, told us that before the Revolution, or the "liberation" as the Chinese call it, forty-nine households had lived there, four of them landlords, the other forty-five peasants. He said that thirteen of these families were forced to sell their sons and daughters for slaves and servants, seven families became beggars and seven died out completely.

Liu was proud of the changes in the Shuang Wang brigade since the area was liberated in 1949 and the commune organized in 1958, and he gave us numerous facts about the brigade and its accomplishments. He told us about their problems and how, by following Chairman Mao's directives, they had been able to solve them. We learned that the retirement age in this commune is fifty-five for men and fifty for women but that, like old people everywhere, "Old Ox," a man of eighty-eight, says he would rather "die in the fields than retire." We were also told about the deaf-mute who helped sink forty-eight water wells to bring the 2,750 mou of land under irrigation and how they experimented to find the best-quality wheat seeds.

From these discussions with many people on many different communes all over China, from watching them and visiting their homes, certain basic things about the life style of a Chinese commune emerged.

Each commune is a self-sufficient unit, as are many of the brigades. Most of them have a stored supply of food grains and the people have a small amount of savings in the bank. The leaders work with the people in the fields. There is a propaganda team attached to each brigade that is responsible for entertainment and education.

[92]

There is one-channel educational television on some communes and government radio in all of them. The people discuss and rediscuss ways of improving their production and their way of life. They like to put on shows and concerts depicting everyday life. The young people are completely involved and are not tempted into drugs or vandalism. They travel to other parts of China to help out when and where they are needed. The families have their own houses (usually built by themselves). The grandparents live with their children and help as much as they can. The peasants work together. There is little privacy. The people have plenty of food and adequate clothing. They pay great attention to their young children. There are enough free schools to give all children an opportunity to complete elementary school and for most to go on to middle school.

Each brigade has a hospital or clinic giving free medical care to workers and to dependents at a nominal cost. Their standard of living, though not comparable to that of the West, is better than it has ever been. They seem happy and secure. Their values are different from American values. Neighbors do not compete for material gain, and there is no profit motive. They work for the collective. They rise early and go to bed early. They are good-natured and hard-working.

Commune Homes

On a commune near Fancheng we visited some homes of peasants and I learned the truth of the old adage "Poverty is a state of mind."

We arrived in the midafternoon when the workers were still in the fields; only the old people, who care for their grandchildren and help with the housework, were at home. They were happy to show us how they lived. The typical house was small, made of white-washed bricks with a gray tile roof. The main room contained a wooden dining table, a few hand-made chairs and stools, and usually had a chest of drawers with a radio on it. The two bedrooms had small wardrobes with mirrors and broad beds called *k'angs*; the beds were warmed by charcoal ovens inside concrete casings and were covered with quilted cotton mattresses and hand-embroidered quilts. Some houses had separate kitchens with iron charcoal stoves; others had the stove in the living room. On the walls were carefully preserved family photos and pictures of Mao Tse-tung.

By any standards this was a humble home, but it was shining clean and better than anything they had lived in before. The genuine pride with which the old people showed it to us was truly touching.

We saw all types of housing in China.

Perhaps the best commune houses we saw were on the Dragon Well tea commune near Hangchow. We were welcomed to the reception room in the home of the former landlord, who we were told now picks tea with the other workers. Classical Ming dynasty furniture, which would make an antique dealer drool with envy, still stands in the large teakwood-walled rooms. Later we walked through the workers' village that has been built on both sides of a wide stream. White adobe houses with gray tile roofs line the cobblestone streets. A gray-haired woman, with the bound feet of old China, stood at the open door of a two-story home. We made her acquaintance and she politely invited us in. Directly opposite the door, so that it could be seen from the street, was an altar table. Over it, a photo of Mao Tse-tung had long since replaced the traditional God of Wealth. A table, some wooden chairs and a washstand stood on the wooden floor in the main room, which was lit by bare electric bulbs hanging from exposed wires. The kitchen had a low wooden table and a large earthen stove with a cooking pot sculpted into the surface. A plump red cat was curled up on a stool, and a blue spittoon stood in a corner. Upstairs were three bedrooms with quaint curtained beds which were typical of that commune. The old lady indicated that the bed with blue-flowered curtains was hers. It was obviously the best one.

Each house had a small garden with flowers and vegetables and perhaps a goat or some chickens. In all the communes, people have their own homes and small private plots to grow vegetables or raise animals for their personal use. Any excess is sold to the commune brigade and the profits divided equally among the brigade members so no one is tempted to become a capitalist.

On the Nan Yuen commune, near Peking, we were shown several storerooms full of surplus food grains to be used in case of war or natural catastrophe. The storerooms had been constructed from the old bricks from Peking's dismantled city wall. People had also used the bricks in combination with stucco to build their homes.

[97]

GETTING AROUND CHINA

The main means of transportation in China are the cross-country railways and the vast network of inland waterways. The highway system is still secondary, although extensive road building is now under way. Air transport is used mainly for people on official missions rather than for freight.

Much of rural China still depends on the centuries-old methods of moving goods short distances by animal and peasant power. In some areas peasants carry their produce to distributing areas in baskets on their arms or attached to both ends of a bamboo *yo* stick slung over their shoulders. The country roads are still full of horse, donkey, ox and even camel carts carrying agricultural goods and building materials. Occasionally a loaded truck honks by, giving loud notice to the beasts of burden that their days are numbered.

There are an estimated 300,000 state-owned trucks which haul almost 30 percent of China's freight over her network of good and bad highways. Most main roads and all roads in urban areas and for about eighty miles around are paved, but many others are still dirt or gravel and heavy rains often make them practically impassable. However, the railways are almost always dependable.

Most progress has been made on the cross-country railways, which have existed since the late 1880s and are the main means of transportation. They now run to almost every part of the country and provide vital links from seaports and inland cities to industrial and agricultural areas. Passenger trains are clean and modern, and invariably run on time. Some of the passenger trains, like the one from Hangchow to Shanghai, have air-conditioned double-decker carriages with plush reclining seats. Formerly the trains were loaded onto ferryboats to cross the large rivers, but now bridges have been built in Nanking, Canton and Wuhan.

Almost as important as the railways is the picturesque network of inland waterways which link China's important industrial and agricultural areas. These include the main rivers, their tributaries and thousands of miles of man-made canals connecting remote areas to the central systems. They are filled with barges, sampans and junks of every size and description. Some are run by diesel engines while others are dependent only on their colorfully patched bamboo-ribbed sails to carry them along the waterways.

Canals run for thousands of miles. The oldest and longest is the Grand Canal, dug over two thousand years ago. It runs six thousand miles. In cities like Soochow and Wusih the canal is crammed with trains of barges conveying local as well as international traffic. In the countryside, canals are hidden by wheat fields which, at harvest time, create the unique sight of junk sails gliding over a sea of tall golden wheat. Larger junks sail the

[99]

rivers, carrying mainly grain, rice, coal, building materials and mineral ores.

But the day of the sailing junk is fading as the motorized junk and the more practical but noisier and less picturesque steamships are taking over. Now only about 25,000 of the 93,000 miles of inland waterways are accessible to steamships, but the ships are used widely in freight transportation along the coastal regions.

Foreign ships are banned from China's inland ports, but the seaports, such as Darien, Canton and Shanghai, are open to foreign vessels.

Shanghai is the largest and best-known Chinese port. In the old days it was jammed with foreign trading vessels of all types. Today there are fewer foreign ships and they are interspersed with Chinese-made or chartered vessels, and the Chinese, rather than foreign traders, are reaping the benefits. The Chinese have only recently begun building their own ships. We toured Shanghai harbor on a motor launch and passed two of their six oceangoing ships of ten thousand tons each. We were told they have plans for twenty-thousand- and thirty-thousand-ton ships. They have about two hundred small oceangoing ships involved in freight transport along the coast and nearby islands.

In the cities people travel in a variety

[101]

of ways. Modern taxis, cars and double-decker buses honk through the hordes of bicycles, pedicabs (bicycle-powered rickshas, which are slowly disappearing) and three-wheeled cars that dart around the horse, donkey and ox carts. Peking has almost completed China's first subway. In October 1972 it was not yet open to the public for everyday transportation, but about sixty thousand people a day went sightseeing for two cents a ride. We took a ride in the front car. The conductor plays revolutionary music on tape as the train whizzes through fourteen miles of tunnels. The sightseeing consists of sixteen palatial underground stations, all constructed in various-colored marbles from Yunnan, near the China-Burma border. There is a pink station, a white station, a black station, a yellow station, etcetera. All are decorated with mosaics, murals and sculpture, and they put even the Moscow subway in the shade.

The operations of the internal airline, CAAC, are limited in scope, but the safety record is good. The Chinese are building small planes, but the airliners, turbojets and jets have been imported from the Soviet Union or Great Britain, and more recently Boeing 707s from the United States. Until 1972 planes flew only in the daytime and in good weather. The main airports are elaborate and comfortable. Restaurants and interesting shops are available. Live concerts are performed to help pass the time, and until recently, when night- and bad-weather flying became possible, there was usually a lot of time to pass. A typical incident happened in 1971 when I joined some other correspondents for a nine-day trip to Sian and Yenan.

Our plane was due to leave "approximately in the morning," so hoping for the best we arrived at the airport at nine-thirty. We waited rather restlessly for two hours before the Chinese told us that the sky over Sian was cloudy and invited us to lunch. We relaxed for two more hours over a multicourse lunch and cold beer. Then we waited while costumed teen-agers on the tarmac waved banners and shouted welcome to an arriving Peruvian trade delegation. Then came a long concert, after which the teen-agers gave another wild welcome to a newly arrived North Korean delegation. About four o'clock we got the word: "Sorry to keep you waiting. The weather in Sian has cleared now. Please hurry!"

We boarded a Russian-made jet and flew off into the clear blue sky feeling safe if not on schedule. A year later I made exactly the same trip on schedule but in the rain.

Making
Politics Work

行政之道

[104]

EDUCATION FOR
THE MASSES

Education is of major importance to the socialist system in China. It is the chief instrument of the class and cultural revolution. When the Communists took power in 1949, they were faced with the incredible task of educating the masses, both literally and politically. If they failed in this, the Revolution would fail, because without the active political support of the people no government in China can succeed for any length of time.

Before the Revolution, an estimated 80 percent of the population was not only illiterate but steeped in ancient customs and superstitious beliefs. Mass education seemed impossible, but things were so bad in China that the peasants knew a change was necessary and therefore were willing to learn.

Since then there have been dramatic changes in education. More than 80 percent of the population is literate. The existing schools were enlarged and new schools were set up in huts, under the trees, in the fields, anywhere and everywhere.

In Yenan we visited schools in the caves where the People's Liberation Army had its headquarters during the Revolution. During recess the army's former training ground rings with the noise of children jumping, racing,

playing Ping-Pong, basketball and the games schoolchildren play everywhere.

Their studies, however, differ in that besides their basic curriculum of reading, writing and arithmetic, they also study the meaning of socialism and the philosophy of Mao Tse-tung, and are expected to share in productive labor.

Education in China must serve politics and be combined with production. It is divided into primary, middle or high school, and schools of higher education including colleges, universities, and technical institutions. Nursery schools are available but not compulsory. Children start school at seven years of age. Their curriculum consists of revolutionary literature and art; politics and language; arithmetic; physical education; military training; and some productive labor. The schools are supervised and financed in the cities by the Neighborhood Committees, in the rural areas by Production Brigades and in factory complexes by Industrial Production Units.

The party's education policy is set by the Central Committee and administered through the Ministries of Propaganda and Education.

As in other countries, school is from Monday to Friday, with weekends free. All primary schools are within walking distance of the students and instead of "car pools" they have "walk pools," in

which the mothers take turns walking the neighborhood children to school. Nursery school tots are sometimes put in wooden carts and pulled to school by the mothers on bicycles. School usually starts before breakfast at 7:30 and lasts until 10:00 A.M., when they break and return home for their morning meal, although some schools in the cities have canteens where the children can eat. The children return to school from 11:00 A.M. to 2:00 P.M., when they go home for the day. After their afternoon meal they are expected to participate in light work projects designed to teach children the various tasks involved in production. Then after play time and the evening meal, they do their homework.

[109]

After six years in primary or elementary school, the students go on to junior middle school, where the hours remain the same, but physics, chemistry, higher mathematics and geography are added to the curriculum. They are also expected to take an active role in helping with the work. In the cities, they learn from experienced workers and participate in building projects and light industry. In the country, the older peasants teach the children how to help with the animals and crops.

By senior middle school, the students devote half their time to productive labor and the other half to academic studies. Since the Cultural Revolution, the complete middle school course has been shortened from six to five years.

The schools are often run in coordination with factories, workshops or agricultural centers where the students work. Thus they contribute to overall productivity, earn their own keep and help support their schools.

After the Cultural Revolution there were no competitive examinations in the Chinese lower school system, but they have recently been reintroduced. Each student is encouraged to do his best and is judged on effort and attitude rather than exam results. Senior middle school graduates from city schools are usually sent out to the countryside to work with the peasants before returning, if needed, to industrial jobs in the cities.

Graduates from country or agricultural middle schools are assigned jobs, usually in their own areas. They are expected to apply their knowledge and pass it on to their fellow workers. When possible, they have a choice of both the area and the work they prefer. Only about 15 percent of them go on to universities. The Chinese have a different attitude toward higher education than we do. The immediate need of the country is for skilled workers and technicians. They see no need for over-education: for a man who harvests rice or builds bridges to be a university graduate, or for a country doctor to be a heart specialist.

HIGHER EDUCATION

Perhaps the greatest change resulting from the Cultural Revolution that began in 1966 is the attitude toward higher education in China.

The shock troops of the Cultural Revolution were the Red Guards, revolutionary organizations formed by the students and some teachers in the universities and high schools. They were told by Mao Tse-tung that the basic things responsible for the deviations in socialist development were the so-called *ssu chiu* or Four Olds—old culture, old ideas, old customs, old ways.

It was felt that the Four Olds hindered progress in all aspects of society, but mainly in the educational system. To eliminate them required criticism of, rebellion against and eventually re-education of the leaders in society, party and government who they considered to be following the "road to revisionism" or old bureaucratic ways, which could eventually lead back to "capitalism" and the highly structured class society of the past. All individuals were encouraged to look into themselves, as well as at their teachers, to search out and banish any tendency toward private gain or personal vanity that would cause them to hold individual values above the collective cause of building a better China for all.

When the Red Guards began the campaign to purge anti-Mao elements across the country, the high schools, the universities, the art and technical institutes were closed for a reassessment of curriculum and the whole educational system. It was felt that the university teachers and students, the so-called intellectuals of China, were getting out of touch with the people and that basically the university system, instead of working for the good of the socialist system, was drifting away from it. China is particularly sensitive to this situation because for centuries during the days of the "intellectual aristocracy" there was a large gap between the intellectuals and the workers. The old mandarin scholars felt superior, looking down on manual labor, and often grew their fingernails several inches long to show that the only work they could do was to hold a calligraphy brush.

The Chinese Communists feared that unless the educational system was brought closer to reality, the old attitudes would again assert themselves, widen the cultural gap and hold back progress.

The schools of higher education were closed for over two years in an attempt to reshape them to fit the essential needs of China's society. They were decentralized and many of the technical institutes were relocated so that the

students could combine their book knowledge with practical application by working closely with experienced workers in agriculture, mining and industrial facilities.

By 1970 many of the scientific and technical institutes reopened, but most of the students who were swept out of their classrooms during the Cultural Revolution and sent to the countryside to "reform themselves through labor" were not in attendance. They stayed in the countryside. Little is known of what has happened to these victims of history who were caught up in the convulsions of the Cultural Revolution. In the Willow Grove brigade of the Liu Ling commune near Yenan, I met some of these student workers and learned what had happened to the 24,000 students transported from their schools to the Yenan region.

I was told by Hsi Huai, vice-chairman of the Yenan Revolutionary Committee, that over one hundred had joined the Communist party and about one thousand were members of the Communist Youth League. He said that the students serve, as well as learn from, the peasants. Seven thousand are working as scientists and 1,200 are teachers or "Barefoot Doctors"—those social workers who are trained in first aid and basic health subjects. Three hundred have joined the People's Liberation Army; 1,400 have been transferred to industry, finance or trade; 2,400 have been assigned to supervise and work with the others, who work as peasants in the fields or do manual labor.

Miss Chou Yu-fung, an attractive twenty-one-year-old from Peking, is one of the students now working as a peasant.

"It was difficult at first," she said. "The living standard in Peking is higher and just climbing the mountains here took the energy out of us. We couldn't tell a potato plant from a tomato plant."

Miss Chou's hair hung in thick braids; she had finer features and a different quality than Yenan peasants.

When asked when she would return to school, she replied, "My main purpose here is to receive re-education. We came determined to take roots and live here. If the country needs us, we will roll up our beds and go."

Only one student from the Willow Grove brigade was chosen in 1971 to go to a university. The new students enrolled in the universities in 1971 were chosen from among the workers, peasants and soldiers, as well as the middle school graduates. They were all over twenty years old and had at least two years of practical experience in the factories and fields. The length of university courses has been reduced to two or three years and they combine study with productive work for both students and faculty.

In evaluating the student's work, political attitude is taken into account as well as exams based on academic studies. The student's report card is a combined assessment by the faculty, fellow students and representatives from the Communist party. The students generally work a thirteen-hour day, split into four hours of academic studies, four hours of manual labor coordinated with their studies, four hours of independent study and an hour of exercise.

At the end of the course, it is hoped that the students will be politically conscious, skilled technicians or scientists able to apply their knowledge and integrate naturally with the less-educated working class.

Art Schools

The schools of fine arts were also closed during the Cultural Revolution and the art students went to the countryside to immerse themselves in the lives of the workers in accordance with Mao's words: "China's revolutionary writers and artists must . . . for a long period of time . . . unreservedly and wholeheartedly go among the masses of workers, peasants and soldiers . . . to the broadest and richest source to study and analyze all the different

kinds of people, all the masses, all the vivid patterns of life and struggle, all the raw materials of literature and art."

The students were sent in an effort to recapture the spirit of revolutionary art which Mao had outlined as early as 1942 in a forum on art and literature held in Yenan. "There is in fact no such thing as art for art's sake, art that stands above classes or art that is detached from or independent of politics," he said. "Proletarian literature and art are part of the whole proletarian revolutionary cause; they are, as Lenin said, cogs and wheels in the

whole revolutionary machine."

The most striking and best-known example of "art for the masses" is an exhibit of over one hundred life-size figures sculptured during the Cultural Revolution and called "The Rent Collection Courtyard." These sculptures depict—in a series of six vivid scenes—peasants, in the semi-feudal days before the Revolution, being forced to pay exorbitant rents to a cruel landlord. Those unable to pay are shown being brutally punished by sadistic henchmen.

The exhibit is reputedly based on incidents that took place on the grounds

of the manor house of a notorious warlord, Liu Wen-tsai, who lived in Szechwan during the Chiang Kai-shek period, and the originals are on display in Liu's former rent collection courtyard. The sculptures are modeled with great feeling and startling realism—taut muscles exude tension and the dark eyes seem to express the fear, pain, humiliation, and finally hope and determination of the peasants as their idealized figures move through the haunting story of the class struggle in old China's countryside. The last scene shows the peasants rising in revolt, seizing weapons from the landlords and marching off to the mountains to join the Revolution.

Reproductions are on display in prominent places throughout China. The most dramatic is in the Forbidden City in Peking. Here the epic figures of the oppressed and exploited peasants are set significantly in a palace called the Hall of Worship of the Ancestors and contrast sharply with the imperial treasures on display in other palaces.

Thousands of students come by bus and truck load to see the exhibition, which has been acclaimed by the Chinese as a brilliant example of how art can serve politics. The sculptures are considered to be important not only because they are artistically strong but because they meet all the requirements of "revolutionary art."

[115]

RE-EDUCATION

During the Cultural Revolution, new kinds of ideological re-education schools, called May Seventh schools, were established for the cadres—that is, Communist party, community and government leaders. The purpose was to study Mao's philosophy, bring the leaders closer to the problems of the people and bridge the widening gap between the workers and the intellectuals. They are called May Seventh schools because on that day in 1966 Mao issued a directive stating: "The intellectuals should be re-educated by the workers, peasants and soldiers." He also said: "Manual labor gives vast numbers of cadres an excellent opportunity to study once again."

The cadres got the message, and officials of all ranks, including diplomats and cabinet ministers, volunteered to be "re-educated." They helped to build their own schools and then worked side by side with the workers and peasants.

In May 1971 we visited the Peking Eastern District Cadre School for Official Functionaries, which had 1,253 student-officials, ranging from twenty-seven to fifty-seven years of age and coming from various walks of life. Mei Kuan-san, thirty-eight, was a deputy chief in the Education Division of the Cultural Bureau in Peking. In the May

Seventh school he was a platoon leader who did field work in the rice paddies. Mrs. Hsu Ying, twenty-six, a schoolteacher, was a masonry worker and helped care for the threshing ground. She was also a member of the propaganda team. Dr. Gen Tsu-tai, formerly a gynecologist in Peking's Department of Housing, now worked as a doctor in the school's clinic. Tien Chi-chen, who was vice-chairman of all the now disbanded trade unions in Peking's Eastern District, made water pails in a school-run factory.

Physical labor is assigned to the student workers according to their age and physical capacity. Care is taken not to strain the older ones. They all continue to receive the salaries from their real jobs. This is paid by the departments they worked in.

The school consists of several one-story buildings built by the students of the bricks and stones from Peking's dismantled city wall. Only the imposing city gates remain in Peking. Besides two small factory buildings and a main hall, there are 311 dormitory rooms. It took the students twenty-one days to complete the buildings. The bed stands are also made from the city wall bricks and the beds from waste planks covered with quilting. They value frugality and point out that their tables were made from old wooden crates that cost only six yuan (about $2.60).

The men and women live from four to six in a room in separate dormitories. There are no families, but students keep in touch with their families by phone and are allowed to go home two days a month. The length of stay varies from six months to two years, depending on their attitudes and how long they can be spared from their own work. When asked how long he would remain, one student replied, "It depends on how I temper myself."

Mr. Wang, the chairman of the school's Revolutionary Committee, explained that they also need to learn from the soldiers and therefore the school is organized in a military way. The students get up at six and do an hour of physical training before breakfast, usually buns or noodle soup, at seven; seven-thirty to eight-thirty is spent studying the works of Chairman Mao Tse-tung.

At eight-thirty they go to work at their various jobs. Most work in the grain and wheat fields that have been planted on virgin land in compliance with one of the principles of the school. Others tend the terraced rice paddies that they have converted from sand dunes. Still others care for the fruit and vegetable gardens, while some clean and feed the animals. Workers also produce water buckets and other farm implements in a factory and make chemical fertilizer. Another activity is

to dig irrigation ditches for their homemade water pump. The only food they buy is pork, but they are still striving to be completely self-sufficient so as not to be a burden on the state.

The student-officials have lunch at twelve noon. It consists of buns or rice plus at least two dishes of vegetables, fish or meat, and costs less than twenty cents. After filling their bowls in a self-service canteen, they eat in their rooms with their roommates.

Mr. Wang said that "some of the officials found it hard to adjust to the spartan life. Some felt that manual labor was a form of punishment. They thought that when they took up the hoe they must put down their pen forever. We have had many heart-to-heart talks with each other," he said, "and with the peasants and workers, and found that we have much to learn from their direct and clear-cut attitude. After studying Chairman Mao's May Seventh Directive, we realize that the cadre school is to educate us to continue the Revolution. Now when they take up the hoes they know they are promoting the Revolution and their own thinking, and when they take up their pens they have a better outlook. They know they are no better than the peasants. Now our faces are tanned and our hearts are red."

There is usually a rest period after lunch, but the day that the visitors came they skipped it to watch an hour-

long show presented by the propaganda team. Under the noonday sun, with the Peking dust swirling and the orchestra going full blast, we watched the students dance and sing and put on skits about their life in the May Seventh school. They looked more like a professional than an amateur group.

After the show they went back to work until 5:30 P.M., when they returned for the evening meal. After another study period, they are free to watch the one-channel television in the common room, sing songs, chat or play Ping-Pong, until bedtime at ten o'clock.

In this country it is hard to understand that these schools are not just reform schools with manual labor as punishment. In a society where the common cause takes precedence, they are viewed more as a refresher course in Maoist ideology that one must go through to become a better member of society. The inconvenience to one's self and family is considered to be of secondary importance.

EVERY SOLDIER
IS A WORKER

In China we were somewhat surprised to see members of the People's Liberation Army in almost every walk of life. They were never armed and seldom marching—but very evident.

When we visited the various city and commune organizations in China, we were always welcomed by leading members of the Revolutionary Committee.

The People's Liberation Army, known as the PLA, is unique in the sense that it is totally identified with the rest of Chinese society and plays an important role in China's economic and political life as well as its national defense. The members of the armed forces are considered by the people to be co-members of an integrated working force struggling to create a new and better China.

The stated aim of the army, which is a unified organization of all land, sea and air forces totaling some 2.8 million, is to defend as well as to serve the needs of the people. Soldiers are often set up as examples to the masses, who are urged to learn from the Red Army's selfless contribution to the state. The army, like all of Chinese society, is politically motivated and its strategy has been shaped by the military writings of Mao Tse-tung. For instance, one influential passage reads:

"The Red Army fights not for the sake of fighting but in order to conduct propaganda among the masses, organize them, arm them, and help them to establish revolutionary political power. Without these objectives, fighting loses its meaning and the Red Army loses the reason for its existence."

Another major task of the PLA is to help in the education, political and otherwise, of the people. Many of the teachers in the universities and medical schools are army men who are also highly qualified for their professional tasks. Army doctors serve in civilian hospitals and in special schools such as the deaf-mute schools and schools for the blind which have been set up in every province of China. They also promote cultural activities with modern political themes, and their touring gymnasts and drama groups perform in the cities and communes.

Besides cultural and political activities, Red Army personnel help in industry, agriculture and civil projects. In the mid-1950s, for example, the army planted over nine million trees in Nanking, which not only changed the appearance of the former Nationalist capital but, they claim, lowered the steaming summer temperature by three degrees. They also engage in irrigation and flood-control projects and in 1963 they dug over 279 miles of canals. During harvest season the fields are full

of soldiers working side by side with the peasants, and on major building projects like roads, railways, bridges and tunnels the army toils beside the veteran workers. In industry, the army is sent in to help meet special deadlines in work production. They also help in historical reconstruction such as repairing the Great Wall and the Imperial Palaces.

When the first rumblings of the Cultural Revolution began in 1965, the system of ranks and titles was abolished in accordance with the policy of establishing a classless society. Technically there are no commissioned officers, but the function of leadership remains. The former officers are now known by their job titles only. Although there are no insignia, an officer can usually be identified by the quality of cloth and the cut of his uniform.

Three years of military service are compulsory for men reaching eighteen years of age. Women may volunteer to serve in the medical, veterinary, clerical and technical services when they are seventeen or older. The women also work with the peasants and workers when the occasion demands.

The Red Army assists in digging air-raid shelters for the people as well as for farm animals and machines, in preparation for a defensive war, but, we were often told, they are not geared

[123]

toward an aggressive war beyond China's own boundaries. There are no Chinese troops on foreign soil and the army is not preparing to fight on a world scale. They point out, however, that they are not afraid of war, but that war against the rest of the world is contrary to the philosophy of Mao Tse-tung and the Chinese Communist party.

Premier Chou En-lai said, "Under no circumstances will we be the first to use nuclear weapons," and our Chinese interpreter, Yu Chung-ching, who is with the Ministry of Information, expressed a common viewpoint when he said, "We will never start a war, but if foreign troops ever make the mistake of setting one hostile foot on China's territory, the whole of China will rise up and swallow them."

If one has observed Chinese society in action, this is not hard to believe because it is obvious that just as every soldier is a worker, the converse is also true, and most workers are prepared to become soldiers if circumstances should demand it.

China Vignettes

中国轻描淡写

[128]

THE TEA AND TEMPLES
OF HANGCHOW

After five weeks of exploring China, my
father, Sylvia and I, along with our
Chinese escorts, reached the resort city
of Hangchow and soon understood why
the Chinese sometimes call it Paradise.
We arrived on May 20, which I remember because the next day was my
birthday. My present was Top, my
husband, who arrived unexpectedly
from Canton to join us.

Hangchow, the ancient garden city
of the emperors and the capital of
Chekiang province, has a history of
over 2,100 years. Marco Polo was one
of the earliest foreign visitors to Hangchow, which was then called Kin-sai, a
name signifying "The Celestial City."
He wrote that "Kin-sai merits from its
preeminence to all others in the world,
in point of grandeur and beauty, as
well as from its abundant delights,
which might lead an inhabitant to
imagine himself in paradise."

Since that time Hangchow has suffered cruelly. It was partially destroyed
by the Mongols in the thirteenth
century and razed again during the
Taiping Rebellion in 1862.

The city has long since been rebuilt.
It is modern and has a population of
720,000. The wide, tree-lined streets
are filled with the usual traffic of
Chinese cities—people walking and

marching, swarms of bicycles, pedicabs
and horse and ox carts. These are all
mixed in with a few cars, noisy trucks
and public buses.

The low buildings, shops and homes
are neatly laid out in square blocks.
The air is refreshingly clean and an
effort to keep it that way is under way.
Most of the factories are situated in
the lush green heavily wooded suburbs,
where vegetation absorbs the fumes.

There are iron and steel works,
chemical fertilizer plants, as well as
machine-tool factories and coal mines
in the area surrounding Hangchow.
Chekiang province, however, is largely
agricultural; of the 3,200 million people
in the province, 2,800 million are
engaged in agriculture. Hangchow is
famous for its tea and silk, but the
province produces mainly food grains
and cotton.

There are few archaeological remains
in Hangchow, but many of the old
temples, villas and palaces still stand
along the nine-mile shoreline of West
Lake. Others are scattered over the
sides of the picturesque mountains that
almost surround the lake.

There is an old Chinese proverb my
father likes to repeat, which is still
heard often in China: "Above is heaven
with paradise; below is earth with
Hangchow and Soochow." (Soochow is
another garden city in the same area.)
The tourist guides, however, point out

[130]

that the city has been a resort for emperors for centuries, but now not only the leaders but the ordinary people as well come to enjoy it.

Secluded lakeside villas are the vacation retreats for top Peking officials, but ordinary tourists can stay in the hotels. We stayed in the Hangchow Hotel and found it spacious and modern, with a first-class restaurant and an interesting gift shop where Sylvia and I bought some exquisitely embroidered wall hangings.

The hotel overlooks West Lake, where we took a gondola to the islands dotted with pagoda-roofed pavilions. There one can wander through the scroll-like Sung dynasty gardens, past the ancient rock gardens and over the moon bridges to the "Park of Orioles Singing in the Willows." By this time all contact with the modern world is lost and one is content to pass the time feeding the golden carp and admiring the blossoms. Later we went to see the golden Buddhas in the "Monastery of the Soul's Retreat." During the Cultural Revolution some "ultraleftist" Red Guards from Peking tried to burn some of these Buddhas, but the Hangchow Red Guards defended the temple. Nearby we wandered through the "Caves of the Morning Mist and Sunset Glow," which are decorated with ancient Yuan rock carvings. There are about 280 figures carved in low relief

[133]

and covered with the mineral patina and green moss of seven centuries. Carved in the thirteenth century, they represent symbolic animals and the pilgrims that brought Buddhism from India to China. Among the figures is the original laughing Buddha, whose mood is so contagious that visitors get carried away and the sound of laughter rollicks from the cave.

In this restful and exotic atmosphere of Old Cathay, we began to forget that we were in the hard-working People's Republic of China. At just about this time, we were whisked away to the East Is Red silk brocade factory, where woven portraits of Mao Tse-tung are churned out by the yard alongside the traditional patterned brocades. This factory produces the silk crafts that are popular all over China. Besides portraits of Chinese leaders they weave Lenin, Stalin and Trotsky as well as epic scenes from the Revolution. A popular one depicts the Communist armies crossing the Yangtze; others include the Great Hall of the People, Mao's birthplace and the Yenan Pagoda.

The factory also turns out many of the rich brocades for export and for exhibition at the Canton Trade Fair. Like China's other industries, the silk factory is growing steadily. In 1949 they had 2,392 square yards of space, 4 workers and 17 hand looms. Today there are 23,920 square yards, 1,700

workers and 300 electric looms. The head of the Revolutionary Committee, however, complained: "We cannot meet the needs of the broad masses, who want more variety and color in their silks."

Besides silk, Hangchow has long been famous for its Lung Ching—or Dragon Well—tea. This tea is grown on the green terraced hillsides of West Lake commune. 1,304 workers live in the 251 houses that make up the workers' village.

The tea is famous because it is "elegant in shape, aromatic in smell and mellow in taste." When Dragon Well tea is brewed with the waters of Running Tiger Spring (which Mr. Chu, our friend and interpreter, jokingly called "Ronning Tiger Spring"), it results in the finest tea in China. It is served in a charming teahouse by an ancient Taoist temple near the spring.

The water has a unique taste, perhaps because of its high surface tension caused by dissolved minerals in the water. While sipping tea, we were amused by a waitress who demonstrated the surface tension by dropping coins into a full bowl of spring water until the water level rose almost a quarter of an inch above the brim.

Chinese and foreigners travel from far and wide to taste this exotic brew. A sweet taste lingers in one's mouth long after the teacup is empty.

THE ANCIENT CAPITAL OF SIAN

The People's Republic of China was built upon the crumbling foundation of one of the world's oldest civilizations—the only one that has lasted into our era.

Since 2500 B.C. a flourishing culture has existed in China. Great dynasties rose and fell long before America was even discovered. The Chinese dressed in silks and ate from porcelain when Europeans were still in the tribal stage. Gunpowder, wood-block printing, the compass and the wheelbarrow were among the inventions of the Chinese. They used paper eight centuries before Egypt and wrote a book on medicine sixteen centuries before Hippocrates.

Although modern China is fully concerned with present-day progress and the future of the country, the Chinese have not turned their backs on their awesome cultural heritage. The historic landmarks of China are being preserved and restored and new archaeological excavations and discoveries are continually being made.

Many of these can be seen near Sian, the ancient capital of China. Here, more than two thousand years ago, the first emperors ruled by the "Mandate of Heaven" over the "Middle Kingdom," which the Chinese regarded as the center of the earth. Masterpieces of enduring art and literature were created in Sian during the golden T'ang dynasty (A.D. 618–906). It was then a cosmopolitan city of travelers, merchants and people of many faiths—Confucians, Buddhists, Taoists, and even Christians and Jews lived together.

Today, on the surface there are few traces of Sian's glorious past, but fabulous museums are tucked away in old temples or behind earthen walls. The oldest archaeological find in the area is the neolithic site at Ban Po village. It was discovered in 1953 when a foundation was being dug for a factory, and excavated in 1957. The site contains the remarkably well-preserved remains of a group of forty-five huts, with foundations in good condition, two hundred storage pits, pottery, tools, six pottery kilns and a graveyard. It is believed to have existed way back in the Yang Shao culture, about 6000 B.C. There is evidence that it was a matriarchal society run on a communal basis. The guides claim it was the world's first communist society.

The Historical Museum in Sian has a unique and beautiful collection of Han, Wei and T'ang dynasty exhibits. There are over three thousand sculptures, bronzes, porcelain and other objects that have been collected from tombs and temples all over Shensi province.

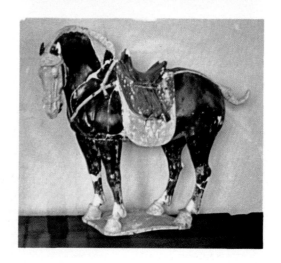

[139]

Near the museum stands a Confucian temple containing the Pei Lin or Forest of Steles. These are 1,095 stone tablets standing on the backs of tortoises or encased in walls. Some date back to A.D. 837. Carved into 114 of the tablets are the texts of the twelve classics (560,000 characters) of Confucius. Other steles contain original calligraphy, memorials, maps and drawings. They are still used by historians, calligraphers and art students, who make stone rubbings.

Another historic landmark in the Sian area is the Big Goose Pagoda. This dates from A.D. 647, when the T'ang dynasty was at its height. The pagoda houses Buddhist sutras that were translated by a Buddhist pilgrim. After the liberation the pagoda was restored and the stairway to the top of its seven stories was rebuilt. The temple contains many fine old idols depicting Buddha's disciples and other charac-

ters, such as the eight fairies, from stories in the sutras.

Big Goose Pagoda is still a working temple, but one sees few youthful or even middle-aged worshipers. According to the constitution there is freedom of religion, but there is strong social pressure on the young people to rely on themselves and the party rather than on religious beliefs. However, we were told that it is generally felt the elderly

are too old to learn and they are left alone to continue practicing their old beliefs as they choose. The old folks often bring their young grandchildren along to the temple, and one sometimes still sees little boys' hair cut in the old-fashioned way. His whole head is shaved except for a topknot of long hair that is left to fool the evil spirits into thinking the boy is a girl and therefore not worth bothering with.

[143]

THE MYSTIQUE
OF YENAN

Flying over the dry terraced hills, looking down on the plateau once covered with hordes of Mongol and Tatar horsemen on their way to conquer China, and later with the remnants of the People's Liberation Army straggling to sanctuary after their grueling six-thousand-mile "Long March," it was hard for me to suppress a feeling of guilt for getting to Yenan the easy way.

In 1934 the Communist leaders and their armies marched for a year to reach Yenan, and the few correspondents, such as Edgar Snow, who had the initiative to get the story had to ride horseback or come at least part of the way from Sian by foot. Since the liberation thousands of student pilgrims have walked for weeks on "little long marches" to visit this "Shrine of the Revolution."

So I came by plane—the modern way to travel backward and relive history —but if necessary I would have walked to experience this tiny mountain city with the ancient pagoda that captured a spirit brought to them by men of vision. I wanted to discover the Yenan mystique for myself. Was the spirit still there?

People who live close to the sea or soil seem to have a special, almost superior quality that arises from an

acceptance of themselves as an essential part of the unity of nature. I found that the people of Yenan have this special quality. To have survived in this poor and ravaged land is to have become part of the dry, eroded earth itself. They are solid, determined, unbending, earthy, dry, hard-working, straight and fair-minded. In the old days they were illiterate and ignorant of world affairs, but they knew who they were and they knew who their friends and enemies were and they remember.

They remember the armies of the warlords who raped and looted and rode away with their food supplies; they remember the Japanese bombs that flattened their houses and killed their people; and they remember the People's Liberation Army, who paid for their food and stayed and helped them plant new crops and irrigate the land and set up schools.

This was from 1935 to 1947, when the revolutionary leaders and their armies arrived after their trek from Kiangsi province in South China. Threatened with annihilation by Chiang Kai-shek's troops, Mao Tse-tung led 90,000 troops on an epic march that dwarfed even Hannibal's journey over the Alps. They crossed eighteen mountain ranges, many of them snow-capped, fought innumerable battles, suffered untold difficulties, lost 83,000 men. The 7,000 survivors arrived in the Yenan area, where they were joined by other Red Army forces. Here the armies regrouped and prepared for the revolution that was being plotted in the caves of Mao Tse-tung, Chou En-lai, Chu Te and other leaders.

The people of Yenan also remember 1947, when Mao and his army of 20,000 men, surrounded by 230,000 Nationalist troops, were forced to leave Yenan. Visitors who are taken to the cave houses to see where the historic dramas took place are given the details of this retreat in such a way that it sounds more like a victory for their hero—the now legendary Mao.

"From March 13, 1947, Chiang Kai-shek's airplanes bombed Yenan day and night," the guide told us. "They dropped bombs into this courtyard and everyone went to the shelter except Chairman Mao. Then his bodyguard picked up a piece of a bomb to persuade him. Chairman Mao took the shell in his hand and said, 'With this you can make a chopper.' . . . On March 16 he met with his troops to explain their inferior position. He said, 'If you save the people but lose the place you finally get both. If you lose the people but keep the place you finally lose both. . . . Now we must leave Yenan, but this action means we will liberate Nanking and the whole country. . . . The occupation of Yenan by Chiang Kai-shek

doesn't mean he triumphs—it is only to lift a rock and let it drop on his feet. In one or two years we will be back forever.'"

The guide showed us Mao's dark cave house, his hard bed and the desk where he wrote his articles by the light of a kerosene lamp and homemade candles. "On March 18, 1947, when the enemy troops were less than seven li away," he recited, "and some of the bandits were actually right in the area, Chou En-lai persuaded Mao to leave. 'But let's eat first,' said Mao. After the

meal he asked his bodyguards to clean the caves and pile up the books. 'It will be nice for the troops of Chiang Kai-shek to read Marx and Lenin's books,' Mao said, and then he left with a victorious face."

The Yenanese peasants are hardly interested in these verbal details, but now—twenty-four years later—they still remember, to the last slaughtered pig and broken window, how the Nationalist troops returned in 1947 to destroy and ravage until the Communists came back on April 22, 1948.

In Liu Ling village, on a commune in the hills, the spokesman for the Revolutionary Committee told us: "In our small village two hundred houses were burned, the doors and windows of sixty families were smashed, they killed and maimed sixty oxen, twenty-four donkeys and thirty-six pigs." His eyes looked pained. "And for no reason—they didn't even eat them. They took all the chickens and we couldn't even hear one cock crow."

Empty mornings . . . This thought alone filled me with deep sadness. In a land where for centuries people have risen at cock's crow, the mornings became empty. A silent indignity.

Since time out of mind the people of Yenan have lived in cave houses carved into the slopes of the dry loessial hills. Now their caves are in the communes. Early every morning the cave dwellers emerge from the snugness of their abodes with buckets of water and willow brooms to sprinkle and sweep, sprinkle and sweep. The swishing noise is punctuated by an occasional rooster's crow or the bleat of a pure white goat scrambling up the ocher honeycombed hills. Their packed-mud terraces soon shine clean and smooth before the wood-latticed windows and doors that front their cave dwellings. If the in-laws live with the family, they have their own cave house

next door. When weather permits, most of the cooking is done outdoors.

Mr. Yu, my interpreter, and I dropped in on a family in the mountain village. The grandfather, Tung Je-lian, fifty-eight, was repairing the high mud wall that separated them from their neighbors. He put down his trowel and looked at us with friendly curiosity. His wife, son, daughter-in-law and grandson all came out of their cave houses and we sat in the sun in the courtyard. They were surprised to find someone had come all the way from America to visit them and answered all my questions with sincerity, but modesty prevented them from volunteering any additional information. They had two small cave houses, one for the old folk and one for the young, that they had built themselves in 1963. Each

house had two rooms dug into the hills and fronted by earth-colored bricks, with large wood-latticed windows and doors to let in the light. Bare light bulbs hung on exposed cords and they were furnished with only the bare essentials, but their homes looked cozy, clean and cared for and they were proud of them.

The grandfather explained that his son and daughter-in-law both worked in the fields. Besides free grain for the five of them they each earned about one hundred yuan each (forty-one dollars) a year. Tung Je-lian was a road maintainer and earned sixty yuan a month, which made him the main provider. His wife helped with the housekeeping and cared for their six-year-old grandson, who also helped a bit with the family vegetable plot, the two pigs and nine chickens they kept.

Both Tung Je-lian and his wife had suffered famine and cruelties from the landlord who formerly owned all of Liu Ling village and the areas around it. They learned to read as adults after the Revolution. Before there was 90 percent illiteracy in Yenan; now only 15 percent of those over forty years of age are still illiterate.

How was life? I wanted to know. Tung Je-lian looked around his well-kept courtyard and said simply, "I remember when we ate roots and wore coarse wool shirts—when the poor

[149]

were set apart and there were two heavens and two skies. We all remember those days."

Standing on the windy and historic plateau six thousand feet above sea level, I looked down at the Yenan River and up at the old pagoda that almost loses its dignity at night when it is lit with gaudy artificial lights, and wondered at the people of Yenan, who, with their plain living and hard work, never lose their dignity and somehow make a stranger feel unworthy. Young revolutionaries added lofty thinking to the spirit of Yenan, but it is people like these who are carrying out the high ideas of building a new China.

An old man relaxed in the sun nearby. His skin was as wrinkled and parched as the dry earth he squatted on. A white towel turban wrapped his head in the jaunty manner of the Yenan people, a silky beard flowed to his chest. I wanted to talk to this old Confucius who seemed to embody the mystique of Yenan, but he put his finger to his ear, pointed to the sky and indicated bombs falling. Then he covered both ears as he relived the blast that had left him deaf. Looking up at me, he felt my sympathy, so he smiled and opened both hands to the sky as if to say, "But I still have the sun."

I left humbled, afraid if I looked back he would disappear. I knew I had seen the spirit of Yenan.

Epilogue

The People of the People's Republic:
A Positive Attitude

后记

Many great changes have taken place in China since I lived there as a student before the Revolution. But the two most important changes, to my mind anyway, are the change from negative to positive in the attitude of the people, and the change in the status of women.

The air of New China is charged with a contagious electricity. Everyone appears purposeful and important. They have a dignity and pride and respect for themselves and their neighbors that did not exist in old China.

In 1946 it was a heart-wrenching experience just to walk down the streets of Nanking because one saw so much filth and misery. Today they have not only cleaned up the cities and raised their standard of living, but they have done it themselves. They no longer resign themselves to fate as they did for centuries, but take fate into their own hands.

On May 1, 1971, my father, Sylvia and I watched the magnificent display of fireworks in honor of May Day. After the spectacular in Peking's Tien An Men Square Dad revealed that he had been "wild with excitement."

"Tonight," he said, "standing there with hundreds of thousands of people, I could feel the very presence of the power that has been released in China by the Revolution."

I knew what he meant; it is a power that is felt by all who go to China.

People power. Millions of people working for a common cause and thinking positively over a long period of time is perhaps the strongest power on earth. For when the Chinese are inspired with the philosophy of Mao Tse-tung—or, as they say, "armed with Mao's thought"—they believe that nothing is impossible. They can move mountains with teaspoons, turn deserts into arable land, change the direction of rivers and harness the tides. All with people power.

Time after time during our travels we were shown things that were once considered beyond the realm of possibility. The Yangtze River Bridge in Nanking, for instance. Both Japanese and American technicians had surveyed the river there in the forties and claimed, because of the conditions of the soft riverbed and the swiftness and great width of the water, a bridge could not be built. When we lived in Nanking, the only way to cross the river was by ferryboat. In 1968 the Chinese completed a double-decker, double-track, rail and highway bridge with a total span of four miles. The chairman of the Revolutionary Committee in Nanking showed us the bridge with pride.

"Foreign technicians could only say helplessly that to build a bridge here is more difficult than to ascend to the heavens," he said. "After the liberation, the Chinese working class succeeded only by relying on our own efforts. True," he went on, "we met with difficulties, but by study and experiments the workers overcame them."

The construction took six thousand bridge builders nine years to build. "We also had lots of volunteers," the chairman of the bridge committee told us. "One day the number reached over fifty thousand." This is only one of thousands of similar examples all over China.

The adulation of Mao Tse-tung and loyalty to the Communist party are difficult for Westerners to understand. They are easier to comprehend when we remember that life in China today, compared to the old days when floods and famine were familiar occurrences, has a new stability which in itself is enough to make the peasants grateful to the political leaders responsible.

All over China we asked farmers and workers above thirty years of age to tell us how their lives had changed since the Revolution. Their answers always stressed a new security, a sense of material well-being, a freedom from oppression and a pride in building a new China. "I never have to worry about my children. I know they will never be hungry as I was," said a woman in the Peng Po workers' settlement in Shanghai. "I have a warm house to live in; before I had nothing," said a bearded old shepherd on the road to the Ming Tombs. "Security," said a miller grinding corn in the Nan Yuan people's commune near Peking. "Before the liberation I was a farm laborer, my food was full of chaff and I slept on the floor. Now I'm working for the Revolution."

A woman working in Cotton Textile Factory Number 3 in Peking, whom Top and I chose at random to interview, told us a moving story concerning her life before the Revolution. At first she was reluctant to speak, but when she saw we were genuinely interested, she told about the difficult life her family had led. One day, when they were unable to pay the rent, the landlord demanded their youngest daughter instead. Her father, who had been warned, had hidden his children. When he refused to reveal their hiding place, the landlord's henchmen took him away. The family found his body the next day; one leg had been cut off. As she talked she began to weep, and the other workers came over to sympathize with her. We said we were sorry that we had caused her to relive this tragedy, but she said it was all right because it was important for us to understand why the people are so grateful to be free from these horrors. This is only one of hundreds of similar stories which gave us an insight into why the ordinary people are so willing to support Mao Tse-tung.

The status of women and the whole family relationship have changed dramatically in China since 1949. In former days women were considered to be and were treated as something less than human. They were entirely at the mercy and whim of men and their corrupt society.

Only two or three girls were tolerated in some poor families; any girl born after that might be drowned, thrown in a pit or abandoned to die in the streets. Girls in wealthy families had their feet bound so tightly, as a mark of beauty and status, that they were crippled for life. They were unable to obtain an education, could be bought and sold by their husbands and fathers, were betrothed as children and compelled to marry in their early teens. After marriage, some became one of a number of wives or concubines who were slaves to their in-laws and often unable to leave their compound.

There is a passage in the *Book of Odes* that shows the attitude toward girls and boys in those remote times:

*Sons shall be born to him; they will
    sleep on couches;*
*They will be clothed in robes; have
    scepters to play with;*
Their cry will be loud.
*They will be resplendent with red knee-
    covers,*
*The (future) king, the princes of the
    land.*

*Daughters will be born to him. They
    will sleep on the ground;*
*They will be clothed in wrappers; have
    tiles to play with.*
*It will be theirs neither to do wrong
    nor good.*
*Only about spirits and food will they
    have to think.*
*And to cause no sorrow to their
    parents.*

This attitude persisted, grew more extreme through the centuries and lingered until the mid-twentieth century. The lives of women in old China were full of unbelievable horror. Suicide became the only recourse and this was often performed en masse. As a result of this cruelty to women, their numbers declined to much less than half the population.

It was not until May 1950—after the Revolution—that they were given equal status, and new marriage laws were passed. Before that, however, some of the new reforms had already existed on paper. In 1911, binding the feet of girls was banned and educational facilities opened up to women, but this was seldom carried out because it depended on the judgment of the family. In 1931, further reforms were attempted, but the feudal customs remained. In 1948, girl infants were still being abandoned in the streets. One Sunday morning in the summer of 1948, I was

walking on top of the Nanking wall and at a particularly high point stopped to look down. There, at the foot of the wall, on the edge of a garbage dump, lay the bodies of three babies who had been thrown to their deaths.

Now this horror has ended. Girls are accepted into the family with *almost* as much joy as a boy and they have equal opportunity for education. All professions and occupations are open to them with equal rights and pay, although there are still a few exceptions to this, such as in part-time work where there is no set wage scale, and in some agricultural communes. Pregnant women get a fifty-six-day maternity leave with full pay. Industrial workers retire at fifty or fifty-five years of age and draw from one-half to 70 percent of their former wages in pension.

The Chinese women have accepted this challenge of equality with vigor and have shown amazing confidence in their abilities. Now almost half the medical doctors and more than half the teachers are women. They participate actively in all levels of society, although men dominate in leadership roles.

The women keep themselves physically fit and use no artificial aids to enhance their appearance. Their fine skins, shining hair and clear eyes come from good health and a vital interest in their work. Various types of face

creams and skin softeners are sold, but no cosmetics are used except stage makeup. Their hands are nearly always delicate and well manicured. This is surprising because the women not only work in the factories and on the farms, but do the housework as well.

Although the marriage law establishes equal responsibility in family life, there are very few men—as in this country—who actually help with the housework.

The new marriage laws read in part: "The arbitrary and compulsory feudal marriage system based on the superiority of man over woman and which ignores children's interests shall be abolished." It was promulgated throughout the land in May 1950 but was effective in some northern districts in 1949. It stipulated that marriages cannot be arranged by parents and must have the consent of both parties. It also bans bigamy, concubinage, child betrothal, interference with the re-marriage of widows and exaction of marriage payments. Husband and wife have equal rights of responsibility and ownership of family property and girls have equal rights of inheritance. Parents have the duty to rear and educate their children, and children are later to support and assist their parents—which I think is rather nice.

It was also stipulated that husband and wife have equal rights for divorce.

The effect of this was sensational. Thousands of subservient women rose up and divorced the smug husbands who had taken them for granted for years. Then many of them joined the revolutionary forces to encourage other women to liberate themselves too.

According to the records of Chiang Chih-chang, vice-president of the People's Supreme Court at the time, during a three-month period in Hsinh-sien 99 percent of all civil cases related to marriage disputes and 81 percent of these marriage disputes had come about as a result of the buying and selling of wives, arbitrary arrangement of marriage by parents, ill treatment of wives by husbands or mothers-in-law, child marriage and bigamy.

Because the feudal marriage system was so deeply rooted, it took years to change the old attitudes. Success was due to millions of workers who made it their business to enlighten and persuade both men and women to change their outlook. The new marriage law has also broken the feudal family system and replaced it with a stronger and more natural family relationship based on mutual love and respect rather than the tyranny of family position and age.

Parents-in-law still live with the conjugal family but are no longer

dictators. They help with household tasks and care for the young children when the parents work. The genuine love that the Chinese of all ages have for their children is a joy to see, and is obvious in the streets and playgrounds. I sometimes found it hard to talk to a woman after she had explained her present work to me, but when I asked about children, and sometimes found I had one the same age, her face would light up and we talked like proud mothers anywhere. If her child was in the nursery school or in a nearby apartment, I was taken there and shown the child with great pride. The result of this affection and attention is a remarkable sense of confidence and security on the part of the children, who seem to exude good health and good humor.

Family planning is practiced widely, and we were told the ideal family has two or three children. This holds true in most urban areas, but as we were reminded one evening during dinner with Premier Chou En-lai, "Old customs die hard."

"There are still a lot of old customs hindering progress and we must carry on," he said. "We must admit there are hindrances and support the women. Not throw cold water on them. On the other hand, women should strive harder."

The Premier continued: "Chairman

Mao once said, 'Don't believe everything they say until you look into it yourself.' In some places it is still like the old days. First there is a girl born, then a second, third, fourth and fifth, until there are nine girls and the wife is forty-five. Only then can she stop trying for a son. Is this equality?"

"As a father of five girls, I sympathize," said my husband.

Premier Chou's thick black eyebrows shot up. "No sons?" he asked.

"He's tired," quipped another guest.

"Oh, no," said Chou En-lai, laughing. "It's Mrs. Topping who is tired. I'm talking on behalf of women."

Women on both sides of the Pacific need all the support they can get, but in the last twenty years Chinese women, considering their starting point, have made more progress than any women in the world. Because of this new equality their enthusiastic support of the Revolution is a source of strength today for the Communist party and the nation.

No one knows the power of the people better than Mao Tse-tung. He created it and used it to the fullest. Mao's power is people power, and his genius lies in understanding how to use it. In 1958 Mao wrote: "Apart from their other characteristics, the outstanding thing about China's 600 million people is that they are 'poor and blank.' This may seem a bad thing, but in reality, it is a good thing. Poverty gives rise to the desire for change, the desire for action, and the desire for revolution. On a blank sheet of paper free from any mark, the freshest and most beautiful characters can be written, the freshest and most beautiful pictures can be painted."

Mao has succeeded in painting his philosophy on millions of these "poor and blank" minds and the result is the awesome power of the people of China.

Mao also wrote: "It is man's social being that determines his thinking. Once the correct ideas characteristic of the advanced class are grasped by the masses, these ideas turn into a material force which changes society and changes the whole world."

This idea of changing society starts with the individual. It is an attempt to transform not the nature of man—for who can say what is the true nature of man?—but the attitudes that have been formed by centuries of predominantly selfish thinking. It is an effort to bring China and her people out of a jungle society where it was survival of the fittest and every man for himself into a new society with a new kind of person whose aim is to work for a cause higher than one's self—whose ambition is to serve society as a whole rather than one's own lust for power, personal profit and recognition.

This idea is a recurrent theme in Maoist philosophy, and it is achieved through hard work, study and a continuing fight against what the Chinese believe to be corrupting ideas from the old society.

Whether this is an impossible dream is yet to be seen, but it has already brought this great country into the world community on an equal footing and with the respect of all nations. This new attitude has affected not only the Chinese in China but Chinese people and friends of China all over the world, who, whether they agree with the present regime or not, are proud of and feel they can learn from China's experience. Recognition of this human and social experiment in changing man and society into a selfless positive force is one of the keys to understanding China and its people today.

Since the establishment of the People's Republic, Americans and Canadians have had strained relations with China. It was not until 1971 that Canada recognized and exchanged diplomats with China and not until 1973 that the United States and China established "Liaison Missions." But, in spite of the barriers raised by opposing ideologies, fear and suspicion, the peoples of North America and China are now making a new and honest effort to understand each other. Both have come a long way from the distorted notions created by lack of tolerance and contact.

Just how far was brought home to me in October, 1972, during a visit to a theater in the remote mountain city of Yenan, in China's Northwest, known as the "Shrine of the Communist Revolution." During a program of skits and songs from the "Revolutionary Dramas" the master of ceremonies unexpectedly asked Lucy Jarvis, myself and four other members of a visiting NBC Television team to reciprocate by singing them something.

Naturally we began to panic. "No, no!" we pleaded. "We are not performers." But the noise in the hall, filled with local Chinese, had been replaced by an expectant hush; we knew we could not refuse.

So this Canadian with Lucy and three other Americans—David Liu, Jo Ann Goldberg, Bill Reardin—and an Englishman, Bryan Anderson, filed on stage to sing an unrehearsed but spirited rendition of the only song we all knew the words to: "God Bless America." To our surprise, we got a standing ovation, so for an encore we sang "We Shall Overcome," ending with the line, "We shall all be friends someday." A Chinese friend stood up and translated it into Chinese, and before long the Chinese Communists and Western Capitalists were all sing- ing the same song: "We shall all be friends someday."